THE
LONDON
PUB

THE
LONDON
PUB

PETER HAYDON & CHRIS COE

NEW HOLLAND

First published in 2003 by New Holland Publishers (UK) Ltd
London • Cape Town • Sydney • Auckland

2 4 6 8 10 9 7 5 3 1

www.newhollandpublishers.com

Garfield House, 86–88 Edgware Road, London W2 2EA, United Kingdom

80 McKenzie Street, Cape Town 8001, South Africa

14 Aquatic Drive, Frenchs Forest, NSW 2086, Australia

218 Lake Road, Northcote, Auckland, New Zealand

Publishing Manager: Jo Hemmings
Senior Editor: Kate Michell
Assistant Editor: Jessica Cowie
Designer & Cover Design: Alan Marshall
Production: Joan Woodroffe
Cartography: William Smuts
Index: Dorothy Frame

Reproduction by Pica Digital (Pte) Ltd, Singapore
Printed and bound in Singapore by Kyodo Printing Co.
(Singapore) Pte Ltd

Cover & Preliminary pages:
Front cover: The Archery Tavern in Bayswater.
Spine: The Flask in Hampstead.
Back cover left: Ye Olde Cheshire Cheese, off Fleet Street; *centre*: The Dog & Duck in Soho;
right: The Duke of Cambridge in Battersea.
Front flap: The Grapes in Limehouse.
Half-title page: The Richard I in Greenwich.
Page 2: The Cock in the West End.
Title page: O'Reilly's in Kilburn.
Right: Ye Olde Cheshire Cheese, off Fleet Street.
Page 6 top: The Flask in Hampstead; *bottom left*: The Blue Anchor in Hammersmith;
bottom right: The Nags Head in Belgravia.
Page 7 top: Cittie of York in Holborn;
bottom left: The Three Kings in Clerkenwell;
bottom right: The Ship & Shovell near Charing Cross Station

CONTENTS

INTRODUCTION

There have been many attempts to try to understand why it is that the pub is such a peculiarly British thing. I owe my entire career to an attempt to answer this question, but I still do not think I truly know what the answer is. This book tries to offer some explanation of what a London pub is, as well as being a celebration of the best pubs in London. Since a picture is worth a thousand words, we have decided to let the pictures do much of the talking. Chris Coe's excellent photography richly illustrates the sheer variety, individuality, humour, whimsicality, vitality, eccentricity and general oddity that are as characteristic of London pubs as they are of Londoners. We have also tried to put the pub in the context of its surrounding streets, their inhabitants and trades, as a pub is shaped by its surroundings, by the flow of life past its doors, in the same way as water carves the contours of a river.

Below: The Sherlock Holmes (see page 45) is a theme pub with a difference: with great conviction it has recreated the Victorian era — pubs' glory years — using memorabilia of the famous sleuth.

This book is also an historical document — a snapshot of what London's best pubs looked like at the beginning of the 21st century. It is unlikely that the pubs shown will look exactly the same when you come to visit them. There will be subtle changes, repairs to the heavy wear and tear pubs suffer, subtle improvements, a change in atmosphere caused by a change in landlord, something intangible perhaps. It is also likely that at least one of the pubs will have been changed out of all recognition. All I can do, therefore, is to present the pubs to you as they are today, lay out what we know about them as they were, and hope that tomorrow they retain the character and charms that led to their inclusion in this volume.

You might wonder what it was that qualified the 116 pubs in this volume for inclusion over the 5,500 other pubs in London. There was only one criterion used when assessing a pub's merit: I asked myself 'Would you thank me for recommending you to go here?', and I hope that you will.

When asking myself this question I had to have a yardstick against which to measure the pub. There needed

to be some kind of test, and I chose what I call the Dr Johnson test. The 18th-century writer and critic's description of what made a tavern special for him is probably unsurpassable:

> *There is no private house in which people can enjoy themselves so well as at a capital tavern. Let there be ever so great a plenty of good things, ever so much grandeur, ever so much elegance, ever so much desire that everybody should be easy, in the nature of things it cannot be; there must always be some degree of care and anxiety. The master of the house is anxious to entertain his guests; the guests are anxious to be agreeable to him, and no man but a very impudent dog indeed can freely command what is another man's house as if it were a tavern, there is a general freedom from anxiety. You are sure you are welcome; and the more noise you make, the more trouble you give, the more good things you call for, the welcomer you are. No, Sir, there is nothing which has yet been contrived by man by which so much happiness is produced as by a good tavern or inn.*

If, when you enter a pub, you feel uplifted and inclined to agree with Johnson that 'No, Sir', man's other contrivances are as mere fancy compared with a good inn, then the pub has passed the test.

Inevitably such a selection is fairly personal. Another author would certainly have included some other public houses and excluded some contained here. I have attempted to be broad in my selection, to ensure a fair geographic coverage as well as to offer something for everyone.

For me, the chief virtue of a pub is that it can be almost anything you want it to be. Provided you do the landlord the courtesy of buying a drink you can stay as long as you like, be as gregarious or as reticent as you like and be as idle or as studious as you like. You can enjoy the company of all or engage in a solitary reverie. You can talk to strangers, make lifelong friends, catch up on gossip, commit to memory a cracking good joke for later use, hold forth on any subject close to your heart and leave whenever you wish (within opening hours, of course). The pub is egalitarian, libertarian, non-judgmental and subversive. For these reasons alone, I rate it as priceless.

Naturally, there are different types of pub in different places. Country pubs are different from

Above: Thanks to its location on the River Thames at Rotherhithe, The Mayflower (see pages 150–51) was once patronized by sailors, dockers and adventurers to the New World.

Below: The Tabard Inn (see page 121) is London's finest Arts and Crafts pub, and was part of the redevelopment of a whole area of west London in this style.

town pubs. Manchester pubs are different from Birmingham pubs and both are different from London pubs. Within London, East End pubs are different from west London pubs, and mews pubs differ from high-street pubs. London has been expanding constantly for centuries. At different periods it has grown at different rates and in different directions, and the pubs that have been thrown up as a result are shaped accordingly. Pubs also vary because they share a different lineage.

Left: The 17th-century galleried George Inn (see pages 144–45) in Southwark is a national treasure. The former coaching inn has a fascinating history and architectural features that have failed to survive anywhere else in London.

In the period from which our earliest surviving London pubs date, the 15th and 16th centuries, there were three types of 'pub' establishment – the alehouse, the tavern and the inn.

The Inn

The inn was defined by the provision of accommodation, and was separately licensed. It evolved from the custom of pilgrimage, and in Geoffrey Chaucer's *The Canterbury Tales* The Tabard Inn is a prime example. Naturally, the functions of inns grew as mobility increased, so that by the early 19th century the coaching inns were frequently grand affairs, important hot-houses of economic activity engaged in trade and the movement of goods, people and information. Today we have forgotten the high regard in which such institutions were held. The coaching era was a golden age for inns. People up and down the country would set their clocks and watches by the passage of the Royal Mail. The opium eater Thomas De Quincey (1785–1859) noted that coaches would start off from London and York at the same time and invariably meet at a bridge that marked the half-way point on the route.

The nation was hugely proud of its coaches and inns, and when they were killed off by the railways there was a genuine popular appreciation that something rather special had passed away. Only one London coaching inn survives today, The George Inn in Southwark (pictured above).

The Tavern

Taking their name from the Latin *tavernae*, taverns barely existed outside London and the ports until the 15th century. The taverns' heyday was undoubtedly the 18th century, and coincided with the emergence and rise of the new merchant classes who, in London at least, made the taverns and coffee houses peculiarly their own.

Although they sold ale the drink of the taverns was wine. Before the introduction of gin into society in the late 17th century, wine was the only other widely available alcohol, but that was not for the masses. Wine held an ambiguous place in popular culture. Most people never touched it, and it could not be demonized as gin came to be because the Catholic Church had decreed, as early as the 6th century, that communion could only be celebrated with red wine made from grapes.

As a nation, we are presumed to have discovered wine only in the last 25 years or so, but we are poor consumers compared with our 18th-century forebears who downed very large quantities. However, since we were frequently at war with France, its legitimate supply was often uncertain. Our long-standing friendship with Portugal meant that port was the popular tavern drink of the 18th century. Consumed as it was in very large volumes, port can be considered largely responsible for having made the 18th century the era of gout and the skull-splitting hangover.

Taverns survive in a few examples, but were very much a victim of gin, since the effect of gin consumption was to make drunkenness no longer respectable. We tend to forget that for our 18th-century and earlier ancestors drunkenness across all classes was – among the English at least – a very frequent occurrence. Dr Johnson himself is supposed to have remarked on one occasion that, 'All decent people of Lichfield got drunk every night and were not the worse thought of.'

Ale and the Alehouse

Beyond coaching inns, another thing the nation was inordinately proud of was its ale. Ale was hugely important in the development of the country. I personally believe that ale is a necessary precondition for civilization. We know that ale — by which is meant a fermented grain drink — was available in the Tigris and Euphrates valley, the cradle of civilization, at a very early date. Some 1,500 years BC Egyptian students were neglecting their studies and spending too much time in the alehouses of the Nile. We also know that when western civilization expanded, the 'primitive' cultures that were discovered did not have ale.

Consumption of ale is also a distinction between nomadic and non-nomadic peoples, as production requires settlement, and settlement creates added problems of hygiene and pollution as people are spectacularly dirty. Ale was safe to drink because it was first boiled, and then made alcoholic. In this process any pathogens were killed and could not re-establish themselves. With the addition of hops in the early 15th century — when ale (unhopped) became beer (hopped) — the preservative qualities of this safe liquid were enhanced. Ale was a staple, therefore, at a time when any settlement was likely to pollute springs and wells.

Ale was not only a staple drink but an important means of payment under-

pinning the feudal economy. The alehouse was an essential feature of any community, and increased in importance as feudal hierarchies broke down after the Black Death and as brewing in the manor house declined. Ale and the alehouse permitted the growth of communities and with them economic development. Subsequently, a general awareness of ale's importance manifested itself in a national pride in the quality and strength of ale and beer, and this pride was shared across all classes of society until the mid-18th century. This common feeling survived the best efforts of the Puritans to suppress alehouses and the general enjoyment of anything 'profane' in the 17th century, and started to evaporate only with the introduction and popularity of gin.

Under the Influence of Gin

The pub as we know it today is a direct descendant of the rude alehouse, shaped by exposure to gin. As part of his anti-French policies, William III (1650–1702) popularized gin in order to reduce the popularity of wine, but succeeded only in making the nation drunk. So, with gin came the revelation that there was an alcoholic drink that was actually bad for people. The impact of this on the 18th-century mind, conditioned as it was by hundreds of years of faith in the virtues of ale, we cannot start to comprehend, and all pubs everywhere have been affected by this profound truth.

The 1740s were the worst years of the first gin fever. It

Above: William III (also known as William of Orange, 1650–1702) opposed the territorial ambitions of Louis XIV of France in part by popularizing gin in preference to wine.

Right: The famous illustration Gin Lane *by William Hogarth (1697–1764) depicted the horrifying effects of gin on the populace of London.*

Above: George Cruikshank (1792–1878) was the most eminent political cartoonist of his day, and was particularly famous for his etchings in support of the Temperance movement, such as this bawdy scene entitled Life in London (1821).

was immortalized by William Hogarth in his famous prints *Gin Lane* and *Beer Street*, in which he contrasted the effects of the foul, poisonous, adulterated gin that stupefied people and rendered them incapable of work with the hearty jollity that came from honest and nutritious beer. Hogarth was making a point to a populace who understood his message painfully well. Between 1749 and 1751 the population of London was estimated to have fallen by over 9,300 as a result of gin consumption, confirming the prescience of those fears expressed around the turn of the century: 'Tis a growing vice among the common people and may in time prevail as much as Opium with the Turks, to which many attribute the scarcity of people in the East.'

The fall in population was also a result of a high death rate accompanying a low birth rate. At the time there were no major outbreaks of disease, London's population density was falling and people's diet was improving as corn prices were low and there were few bad harvests. Meat was fairly cheap and there was a rapid expansion in the market garden industry. There were also improvements in the sanitary facilities in the metropolis. All these factors should have conspired to produce a population explosion, and the fact that the population did not increase, but actually fell, was blamed unequivocally on gin.

Tamed By Temperance

By causing such massive trauma to the nation's health and wealth, gin paved the way for the Temperance movement and anti-drink lobbies of the 19th century.

The effect of the first gin fever was to detach the middle and upper classes from the universal enjoyment of drink and to create an increasing intolerance of over-indulgence. By the time the second gin fever broke out in the 1830s, sufficient time had elapsed (not to mention other social transformations such as the Industrial Revolution with all that that meant for social values, living conditions and class differences) for the response to be much more earnest and organized.

The Temperance movement of the 19th century was a massive political campaign. By the late 19th century and early 20th drink was a political issue. W. E. Gladstone, leader of the Liberal Party, was famously 'borne down in a torrent of gin and beer' in the 1874 election. The Liberal and Tory parties were split on pro-Temperance and pro-trade lines. Opposition to the draconian and hugely unjust 1908 licensing bill, which had an affect on the activity, appearance and number of pubs, provoked demonstrations in Hyde Park that attracted 800,000 people.

One effect of the bill was to bar individuals with brewing connections from sitting on magistrates' licensing benches, while individuals with Temperance sympathies actively insinuated themselves onto benches. Justices of the Peace, who ever since 1255 had been tasked with regulating the supply of drink to ensure that there was an adequate supply of ale for the nation, started flagrantly to abuse this power by trying to restrict the availability of alcohol. Benches acted outrageously, making capricious decisions, often *ultra vires* and usually without regard for the loss of livelihood of the publican and his family. Not for nothing was the activity of the benches called a 'tyranny'.

The effect of this was to make licences increasingly rare. Those places whose licences were not suppressed had to be made respectable in order to avoid suppression. At the same time, in the 1880s, the first of the brewery flotations took place – starting with Guinness. Its 1886 flotation was over-subscribed some 50 times and raised a staggering £6 million. Brewing companies rushed to float. They merged and bought each other up in order to become better flotation prospects, and numerous successful flotations meant that the trade was awash with money.

The London Pub

In London there had been a gentlemanly system whereby brewers did not tend to own pubs, but secured their access to the market by the vastly cheaper ploy of 'tying' publicans to them by way of loans. Outside London, breweries increasingly owned their pubs, a practice that had come about as a reaction to endemic adulteration at the start of the 19th century. The newly cash-rich brewers, and those from outside London in particular, started buying London pubs. On the defensive, the London brewers started buying them too. The result was an orgy of spending that varied in nature according to the government of the day.

When the Liberals were in power the tendency was to refurbish public houses to attract custom in an increasingly competitive market and improve the house in order that magistrates would be more likely to suppress another. Under Tory administrations licences were felt to be more secure and larger numbers of pubs would be bought by brewers and more public houses would be commissioned from architects and builders. The two-party system, therefore, was very effective at completely changing the appearance of public houses. Expansion under Tories would be followed by retrenchment under Liberals, which would lead to increased pressure to buy under Tories. The whole together created a highly inflationary spiral.

The Crown in Cricklewood Broadway, for example, was sold in 1873 for £2,000. It was sold again for £5,000, then £15,000, £32,000, £42,000 and in 1898 it achieved £86,000. The upward spiral was a speculator's bonanza, and the entry of non-trade interests fuelled inflation. The Cannon Brewery of Clerkenwell spent £1,363,010 on acquiring 125 pubs between 1893 and 1898, paying maximum amounts in each year of £23,000, £24,500, £28,200, £50,000, £55,000 and £86,000, in addition to the £250,000 spent on rebuilding or refurbishing their new acquisitions.

Once acquired, pubs had to recoup the inflated prices that had been paid for them. In order to do this they had to attract more custom, and to attract more custom the pub had to be rebuilt or refurbished. Frequently, pubs that had been redecorated in the late 1880s would be further redecorated or rebuilt in the 1890s. The net effect of all this was to ensure that very few surviving town pubs date back much earlier than the 1880s. The other effect was to make the speculation and Temperance-driven spiral unsustainable. In the late 1890s an increasing number of bankruptcies among publicans and brewers who had spent more on their pubs than they could ever hope to recover led to an almighty property crash.

Beer Today, Gone Tomorrow

The consequences of this crash were two-fold. Firstly, it meant that there was very little pub building after around 1898, so while London pubs may date from any of the last six centuries, their surviving fabric is likely to date from a relatively short period – the 1880s and 1890s.

The second is that the bankruptcies led to a further concentration of pub ownership. For most of the 20th century, London was characterized by a very small number of free houses competing with ever larger combines of brewers offering an ever smaller selection of beers.

This came to a head in 1989 when the Monopolies and Mergers Commission produced its report, 'The Supply of Beer', which concluded that the big brewery

Below: A cartoon from an 1890 edition of the satirical magazine Punch *tells the story of the increasing influence of brewery shareholders on the future of public houses in the late 19th century.*

Above: London brewery workers pose for a photograph c.1900 with the tools of their trade, including tubes for filling the barrels and hammers for bunging them. When this photograph was taken, brewing was Britain's largest export industry, with products taken all over the globe.

combines were effectively running a monopoly that operated against the public interest.

The history of the British brewing industry since that fateful report has been a sorry one, in large part because the politicians made a hash of implementing the report's recommendations. The result is that today, instead of most pubs being owned by brewers, most are owned by pub companies that are little more than property management firms.

The old brewery firms were in the business of selling beer and in order to do that they needed pubs. They therefore had a vested interest in ensuring that the pub fulfilled its traditional functions in the community, and consequently were fairly philanthropic, as indeed are those brewery firms that still do own pub estates – in London they are principally Young's and Fuller's, though others like Shepherd Neame (Kent), Hall and Woodhouse (Dorset), McMullens (Hertfordshire), Adnam's (Suffolk) and Sam Smith's (Yorkshire) also have small toe-holds in the London market. Today's pub companies do not need to sell beer; they need only one thing – a guaranteed income stream to service their debt obligations. This means that if a pub can generate more cash in the short term by being sold off as a private house then they will sell it.

This is a particular problem in the countryside where it is estimated that six pubs a week are closing and that 50 per cent of Britain's rural population has no easy access to a local pub.

In the town this means that if a pub can generate more revenue as a car-park, then it will become a car-park. It also leads to the creation of superpubs. If there are only so many pounds in people's pockets earmarked for spending in the pub then it makes little sense to run 10 pubs in any community when encouraging them all to go to just one or two pubs is so much more profitable. This means that pub company investment is channelled away from 'community' pubs towards larger 'town centre' venues. It then becomes usual for the community pubs to be sold or closed because they have become unviable.

This is creating a highly undesirable state of affairs. The pub, far from being a centre of the community, where common and local identities are forged, where civic values are instilled, where much local philanthropy takes place and, most importantly, where people still have the increasingly rare chance to engage with people of other generations, is increasingly becoming homogenized. High streets increasingly resemble each other, lined with identi-kit branded pubs aimed at a very narrow market segment and offering an equally narrow, cost effective range of core products.

Most remarkably, the social consequences of this shift in pub culture over the last decade cause very little popular debate. Indeed, the Labour government started its second term in office in 2001 by immediately reneging on its election pledge to reform Britain's arcane licensing laws, which cause so much bemusement to visitors and tourists who come from countries where the law does not oblige pubs to shut at 11pm.

This is not to say that the pub's ills all stem from the last decade. Far from it. Our licensing laws date from the First World War when drunkenness, especially among the populations working in essential industries such as ammunitions manufacture, was a threat to the war effort. On 29 March 1915, the Chancellor of the Exchequer, David Lloyd George, declared, 'Drink is doing more damage in the war than all the German submarines put together... We are fighting Germany, Austria, and Drink, and the greatest of all these deadly foes is drink.'

The Beer

Despite these concerns for the future of the British pub, there are still many good pubs to be found in London and the rest of the British Isles. Only 116 pubs were selected for this volume, and it was a hard job to choose so few as many, many more qualified. Just as a demand for 'real' pubs still exists, so does a demand for real ale — that is, beer that undergoes a secondary fermentation in the container from which it is served, and which is not normally pasteurized or injected with additional gas.

There are some delightful beers to be had in London pubs, and, while it is the case that the peculiarities of London pub ownership mean that beers from only a handful of brewers out of the 500 in the United Kingdom are widely available, a pint of well-kept bitter is one of the great gastronomic delights London has to offer.

Fuller's London Pride is the beer you are most likely to come across in the pubs in this book, as a result of distribution deals which take it way beyond the west London heartland of the Fuller's estate. Slightly behind London Pride, in terms of availability, is Adnam's Bitter, which again is fairly ubiquitous as a result of distribution deals. In third place is Young's Bitter: this is because a fair number of pubs in this book belong to Young's. In all, excluding guest ales, there are some 36 beer brands available in the pubs in this volume, produced by 17 brewery companies. Interestingly, the national brewers do fairly badly, with only Courage Best having a significant London presence. Brands such as Bass, Tetley, Theakston's and Boddingtons do not have much of a profile in the capital's best pubs, and fare very badly compared with brands from small regional brewers like Harvey's and Brakspears, or the Yorkshire duo of Timothy Taylor and Sam Smith.

So, whichever pubs you choose to visit, and whichever beers you choose to sample, always remember you are supporting a historical institution and partaking in a pastime enjoyed by people from all classes for centuries past.

Drink and be happy!

Peter Haydon

Above: The Chiswick brewery company Fuller's delivered its products to its pubs by horse and dray well into the 20th century; this picture was taken c.1920.

Below: Brewery companies have often appealed to new generations of customers by updating the style of their beermats, as this post-war beermat illustrates.

THE WEST END

Soho, Covent Garden, Leicester Square and Piccadilly are all places synonymous with eating, drinking and entertainment, and have been for centuries. The drinking holes of Soho have long been frequented by both die-hard beer and whisky drinkers, such as Jeffrey Bernard, Dylan Thomas and Francis Bacon, and the more refined celebrities who love to quaff champagne at the surprisingly unpretentious French House. Around Covent Garden and Piccadilly the pubs attract the pre- and post-theatre crowds, while those pubs on the roads off frenetic Oxford Street may well be visited by the more adventurous tourist with a thirst who is seeking not only a drink but also some peace, quiet and tradition.

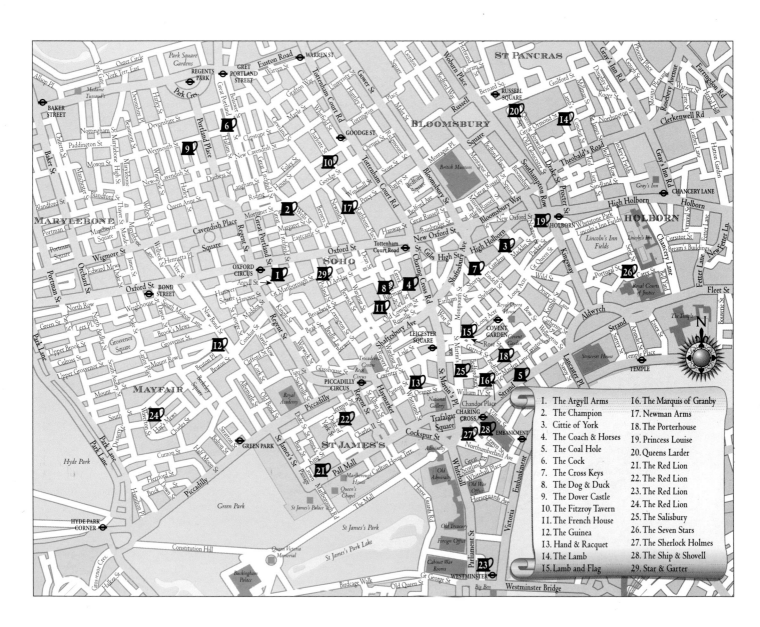

1.	The Argyll Arms	16.	The Marquis of Granby
2.	The Champion	17.	Newman Arms
3.	Cittie of York	18.	The Porterhouse
4.	The Coach & Horses	19.	Princess Louise
5.	The Coal Hole	20.	Queens Larder
6.	The Cock	21.	The Red Lion
7.	The Cross Keys	22.	The Red Lion
8.	The Dog & Duck	23.	The Red Lion
9.	The Dover Castle	24.	The Red Lion
10.	The Fitzroy Tavern	25.	The Salisbury
11.	The French House	26.	The Seven Stars
12.	The Guinea	27.	The Sherlock Holmes
13.	Hand & Racquet	28.	The Ship & Shovell
14.	The Lamb	29.	Star & Garter
15.	Lamb and Flag		

THE ARGYLL ARMS

ADDRESS: 18 ARGYLL STREET, W1
BEERS: TETLEY, FULLER'S LONDON PRIDE, GREENE KING IPA
HOURS: MON–SAT 11AM–11PM; SUN 12 NOON–9PM

Given its location it is to be expected that The Argyll has to treat with the tourist trade on a large scale, and given the splendour of The Argyll passing tourists would be missing out if they did not pop in. The pub takes its name from the Duke of Argyll, one of Marlborough's generals, whose London mansion stood on the site now occupied by the nearby London Palladium. Both this pub and an earlier Argyll Arms dating from 1716 were torn down in the 1860s. The present building dates from 1866, but, unlike many of its contemporaries, it was not remodelled or expanded in the 1880s or 1890s and retains much of its original interior. In fact, one could go so far as to say that it is the best-kept pub of its kind anywhere.

Fine etched and engraved glass splits the pub into a number of booths, affording privacy from strangers in neighbouring booths. To the rear an open dining area offers an excellent view of the magnificently ornate plaster ceiling, as well as an unusual profile of your own head, since it also contains a large number of mirrors.

Voluptuously dark in colour, with a rich mahogany bar running the entire length of the pub, this is a fairly close approximation of what the Victorian pub was like. If you can exercise your imagination, suspend belief and block out the piped music you might just conjure up a similar scene, smokier and smellier, perhaps, with all kinds of Victorian street characters passing to and fro — bowler-hatted Hackney drivers, flat-capped costermongers, top-hatted gentlemen, all busily engaged in the hectic task of relaxation.

Left: The Argyll Arms is a must-visit pub for its exceptional period features and relative tranquillity considering its proximity to frenetic Oxford Circus.

Previous page: The Cross Keys, near Covent Garden, is surrounded by magnificent foliage. The sign above the door depicts the crossed keys of St Peter: it is not unusual for pubs to have religious names or connections.

THE CHAMPION

◆

ADDRESS: 13 WELLS STREET, W1
BEERS: SAM SMITH'S OLD BREWERY BITTER
HOURS: MON–SAT 11.30AM–11PM; SUN 12 NOON–10.30PM

There is no more appropriate name for this pub, which is just one huge celebration of excellence. However, beware, as all is not what it seems – very little in this 'Victorian' boozer actually predates 1953.

The pub was originally named after Tom Figgs, an 18th-century prize-fighter who was the first to be recognized as a 'champion', and the building stands on the site of a booth where Figgs made a living teaching boxing. The pub fell into disrepair in the post-war years – as did many – and it was refurbished in the 1950s in the Victorian style, with Toby jugs on the walls and a collection of Victorian china spirit and wine barrels overhead.

The pub, however, was once more allowed to run down over the years, until it was rescued in 1989 by the Yorkshire brewery firm of Sam Smith's. The brewery really went to town on the pub, installing stained-glass windows by Yorkshire artist Anne Sotheran to outclass those of many an English country church. The windows celebrate the best of British in a range of endeavours, and individuals commemorated include, among others, the explorer David Livingstone; the first cross-Channel swimmer Captain Matthew Webb, who died trying to swim the Niagara Falls; Edward Whymper, conqueror of the Matterhorn; the Earl of Mayo, Viceroy of India; the cricketer W. G. Grace; Florence Nightingale, Crimean war nurse; and Bob Fitzsimon, champion boxer. All in all an eclectic bunch, though champions all. Meanwhile, champion heavy-horse stallions are commemorated on the stairs, and pioneers in the worlds of science and engineering are remembered in the upstairs bar and dining room.

The Champion is a hugely successful pub, not least for being a very expensive practical joke in that the majority of its customers will believe that it is an authentic Victorian or Edwardian pub. There is a clue, however: Captain Bertie Dwyer, erstwhile president of the St Moritz tobogganing club and hero of the Cresta Run, died only in 1967, and this is recorded in the 'Victorian' stained glass.

Above right: Although not entirely as authentic as one may think from first appearances, The Champion is nevertheless most definitely a typical Fitzrovia pub.

Right: Careful restoration work by Sam Smith's Brewery has resulted in a very distinctive interior with an impressive bar and delicate light fittings.

CITTIE OF YORK

ADDRESS: 22 HIGH HOLBORN, WC1
BEERS: SAM SMITH'S OLD BREWERY BITTER
HOURS: MON–SAT 11.30AM–11PM

If you have visited the Princess Louise (see page 37) on High Holborn and viewed its Victorian opulence, then another 'must visit' destination is Ye Olde Mitre Tavern (see page 75) at the other end of Holborn. En route drop into the Cittie of York for a taste of the bogus and the bizarre.

This pub is an early example of the reaction to the gin palace architectural style that was to develop into the mediocre Brewers' Tudor of the 1920s and 1930s. In the inter-war years the brewing industry was so desperate to gentrify pubs in order to 'out-Temperance' the Temperance movement that it decided that a pub could resemble anything that wasn't a pub. This establishment's 'Merrie England' overtones were clearly an inspiration for much of what followed.

The amazing thing about the Cittie of York is that it resembles nothing and everything. The frontage is reminiscent of the great medieval coaching inns, such as the Angel at Grantham or the George at Glastonbury, while the long main bar cannot seemingly decide whether it is a porter tun room, a baronial hall or a real tennis court. Tudor bay windows sit over Art Nouveau arches. The booths along the east wall are a cross between church confessionals and Great Western Railway train compartments, and throughout all runs a mysterious 'HR' motif.

The most striking features of the long bar are the wine *tonneaux* ('casks'), which allegedly saw service until the start of the Blitz when they were drained and never refilled. Their presence is ironic as butts and casks of similar size were very much a feature of original 1820s and 1830s gin palaces – the precursors of the later Victorian style that the Cittie of York was a reaction against. Sadly, no original gin palace casks of this size survive anywhere.

There has been an inn on this site since 1430, but it has only been known under its present name since 1979, when it was acquired by the Yorkshire brewery Sam Smith's, which has done more to preserve London's pub history and heritage than any London brewery. If the long bar is not to your taste then try the small wood-panelled front bar or, if you are eating, the cellar bar, both in very different styles again.

Below: With its baronial hall-cum-cloister interior, the Cittie of York must rank as one of London's most eccentric public houses.

THE COACH & HORSES

◆

ADDRESS: 29 GREEK STREET, W1
BEERS: FULLER'S LONDON PRIDE, MARSTON'S PEDIGREE, BURTON PALE ALE
HOURS: MON–SAT 11AM–11PM; SUN 12 NOON–10.30PM

Soho without The Coach & Horses would be unthinkable. If buildings can epitomize a place and time then Soho is Ronnie Scott's Jazz Club, The French House (see pages 28–29) and The Coach & Horses. Ronnie Scott, the saxophonist who did more than anyone for jazz in the United Kingdom, passed away in 1997, but lives on in his club. The journalist and professional drinker Jeffrey Bernard also passed away in 1997, and he lives on in The Coach & Horses.

The pub is largely unchanged since Soho became the haunt of 1950s writers and artists, many of whom had decamped from The Fitzroy (see page 27). In Soho's run-down and sleazy streets they found the ideal place to live, hide, create, drink and generally get away from the rigidities and austerity of post-war London life. Soho was made by the regulars of The Coach & Horses. Two names shout at you, literally, from the walls of this wood-panelled pub which has, in many respects, the feeling of a 1950s ice-cream parlour – Norman Balon, the landlord, and Jeffrey Bernard. Both are immortalized in the 'Regulars' cartoons produced by another longstanding Coach regular, the illustrator Michael Heath. The cartoons ran for many years in *Private Eye*, and the magazine's often cutting editorial lunches still take place at The Coach.

Norman Balon is famed as the rudest publican in London, although older Sohoites say that underneath it all he has a heart of gold. His distinctive and surprisingly genial features can be seen smiling out from photos on the walls of a few other pubs in this volume.

Jeffrey Bernard, whose fame extended way beyond Soho as a result of his weekly 'Lowlife' column in the *Spectator* where he chronicled his gradual and rather pathetic decline in a beautiful prose style,

was a regular for decades. He is one of very few people to have had a play written about him during his lifetime – *Jeffrey Bernard is Unwell* by Keith Waterhouse. Jeffrey's photo hangs on the wall next to the ladies' toilet; he would have liked that.

Above and below: The Coach & Horses was the epitome of Soho during the area's golden years of the 1950s and 1960s, and this spirit survives there still.

THE COAL HOLE

ADDRESS: 91 STRAND, WC1
BEERS: TETLEY, FULLER'S LONDON PRIDE, ADNAM'S BITTER
HOURS: MON–SAT 11AM–11PM; SUN 12 NOON–5PM

This unusual pub occupies a frontage of the Savoy Hotel building and is full of mysteries. What is the meaning of the SWL motif repeated in its leaded windows? Who are the maidens represented picking grapes on the frieze round the walls? What are the three strange objects in stained glass over the side entrance – cabbages or hearts? What is the significance of the three painted coats of arms bearing the names Beaufort, Savoy and John O'Gaunt? Why is the pub called The Coal Hole? Sadly, no answers are to be found in the pub. One can learn, however, that the actor Edmund Kean founded the Wolves Club for fellow actors here in 1815; and no doubt he retired here after his theatrical exertions at the nearby Lyceum, which he helped make famous.

The present fabric dates only from 1904, hence the slightly Art Nouveau feel to the place, which sits oddly with the equally slight medieval tone created by the leaded windows, stone and dark beams. The date is surprising in itself, since during the 1880s and 1890s there was a massive pub price explosion which inevitably led to a crash, with the result that around 1904 very few pubs were being built (a notable exception being The Black Friar (see pages 50–51)). Its date can be explained by the fact that it was part of the large Savoy development. Indeed, the motif in the windows probably stands for Savoy Wine Lodge.

The pub takes its name from an early 18th-century landlord known as the singing collier, who would encourage customers, including cartoonists Gillray and Rowlandson, to join in with the musical entertainment. The original pub was demolished in the 1880s to make way for the Savoy Hotel, but when the wine lodge was opened in almost the same location Londoners typically continued to refer to it by its old name, so The Coal Hole it remained.

Above left: The entrance to The Coal Hole mimics the canopies of the theatres that appear on the opposite side of the Strand.

Left: The Coal Hole's interior is a hotchpotch of styles and themes, creating something of an enigma.

THE COCK

◆

ADDRESS: 27 GREAT PORTLAND STREET, W1
BEERS: SAM SMITH'S OLD BREWERY BITTER
HOURS: MON–SAT 11.30AM–11PM; SUN 12 NOON–10.30PM

Great Portland Street is at the heart of London's rag trade, which extends off it along Margaret Street and Great Castle Street. The Cock, being well situated towards the Oxford Street end of the thoroughfare that bisects the Portland estate, is a great place to pick up some local history. Should you strike up conversation with one of the regulars, you may well learn that James Boswell – Samuel Johnson's acolyte and inventor of the modern biography – died in a building on the site of what is now 122 Great Portland Street in 1795, or that other famous local residents included the composer Carl Maria von Weber, the libertarian Leigh Hunt and the painter David Wilkie; meanwhile Pagani's – one of London's earliest restaurants – was on the site of number 42.

Oxford Street runs along an old Roman road, and takes its name not because it was known in the 1680s as the 'road to Oxford', but because in 1713 the north side of the road had been acquired by the Second Earl of Oxford, whose daughter married the Duke of Portland, and their family connections provided the inspiration for many of the street names in the area. Oxford Street's history could occupy a book in itself. It was the haunt of Thomas De Quincey, the opium eater; while every day the ruined Harry Gordon Selfridge made a sad figure standing in front of his own store – from which he was banned to stop his lavish ways from bankrupting it.

Both these characters would have known of The Cock, and

Above: The massive Victorian lanterns that hang outside The Cock are among the best-preserved examples in London.

Right: Victoriana still reigns supreme inside The Cock, and although some partitions have been removed, several snob screens remain intact.

today it is still a handsome Victorian pub with many original features. In particular, the pub's snob screens are still in their original locations. These indicate that the pub would have been further subdivided, although a larger than normal amount of partition work survives. The idea behind the snob screen – a small frosted-glass window at head height that could be swivelled open – was that it allowed you to order drinks from the bar staff without your face being visible to customers in other booths or bars. This was of particular concern to the highly class-conscious Victorians, especially those in trade, who would not want their social inferiors or junior colleagues seeing what, when or how much they were drinking. This was especially important during this period as work and home were much more closely intertwined than is now the case: you could not escape back to the suburbs to gain anonymity as you were much more likely to live in the neighbourhood where you worked. In addition, London business life was much more street-focused. In The Cock, however, we can be grateful that the Victorian desire for privacy from prying eyes and gossip created such opulence.

THE CROSS KEYS

ADDRESS: 31 ENDELL STREET, WC2
BEERS: COURAGE BEST, MARSTON'S PEDIGREE, SWEET WILLIAM
HOURS: MON–SAT 11AM–11PM; SUN 12 NOON–10.30PM

In 1101 Queen Matilda founded a leper hospital and dedicated it to St Giles, the patron saint of outcasts. Her prescience was astonishing: St Giles was the parish in which the Great Plague of 1665 started; in the 18th and 19th centuries it was notorious as the poorest parish in London and home to Irish immigrants. In the 19th century the spire of Henry Flitcroft's St Giles-in-the-Fields church was one of the most recognizable and most notorious features of the London skyline. Well into the 19th century the population of this small and self-contained neighbourhood was known to have a life expectancy well below the rest of the metropolis. It was in Endell Street (named after a rector of St Giles), in the shadow of St Giles-in-the-Fields church, that The Cross Keys was built in 1848.

The creation of Endell Street was a much-needed slum-clearance measure. It must have been in the spirit of hope that The Cross Keys — the symbol of St Peter, key holder to the gates of heaven — was named. It was probably in the spirit of protection too, since not even the slum clearances to the north could disguise the fact that Covent Garden to the south was also an area of brothels and whores, who may have used The Cross Keys as a place to pick up customers or stop for refreshment.

Today's pub is a glorious fusion of modern London and Londoners' taste for Victoriana. As far as Victorian clutter goes The Cross Keys is a prize winner, full of authentic bric-à-brac: antique clocks that still tell the time, a cricket bat signed by the legendary Don Bradman, enough copper hanging from the ceiling to make customers wary during a thunderstorm, all interwoven with a newer generation of bric-à-brac — Beatles memorabilia to be precise.

The whole pub is lit by a diffused light that has the feel of gas and cleverly brings out the richer tones and shades of an old London pub. Bright it is not, but hopefully this will not detract from your perusal of the countless treasures housed here. This pub is one of a handful owned by the proprietors of the Sweet William Brewery in Leyton, east London, and is a rare outlet for their microbrewery beers, of which one will be on offer, albeit regularly changing.

Below: The Cross Keys radiates a warm copper glow from the countless pots and pans and eccentric memorabilia that line the walls and ceiling.

THE DOG & DUCK

ADDRESS: 18 BATEMAN STREET, W1
BEERS: FULLER'S LONDON PRIDE, TIMOTHY TAYLOR'S LANDLORD
HOURS: MON–FRI 12 NOON–11PM; SAT 4PM–11PM; SUN 5.30PM–10.30PM

The Dog & Duck is one of a number of Soho pubs whose names refer to the days when the area was a royal hunting ground. Today there are a number of pubs called the Blue Post after the posts in the forest that denoted the boundaries of that hunting ground.

The Dog & Duck's long history has enabled numerous famous people to pass through its door. There has been a pub of this name in this part of Soho since 1743, which means Wolfgang Amadeus Mozart may well have been familiar with it when he lodged with his father and sister at No. 20 Frith Street between 1764 and 1765 (although it is doubtful he was ever a customer, having been only nine years old at the time). In March 1765 Mozart senior placed an announcement in *The Public Advertiser* to the effect that 'Those Ladies and Gentlemen, who will honour him with their company... may... hear this young music master... perform in private, by giving him any thing to play at sight...' Thus it is likely that regulars of The Dog & Duck would have been aware of the young prodigy.

Other illustrious personages who may have patronized the pub include painters John Constable and Dante Gabriel Rossetti. George Orwell is known to have used the pub, and another famous likely customer was John Logie Baird, who used his bedroom at No. 22 Frith Street to give the first public demonstration of television to members of the Royal Institution on 26 January 1926. The apparatus Baird used in the demonstration is now on display in the Science Museum.

The present pub dates from 1897, and contains a large quantity of the highly glazed tiles that were a popular pub decoration of the time. Indeed, it is one of London's best examples of the use of tiled panels: at the back of the pub they resemble hung tapestries and at the front they extend down to the floor incorporating bespoke dog and duck designs. The architect, Francis Chambers, was careful to enclose the exterior in glazed tiles too, above the height of the grey marble on the ground floor. Take a moment to glance up and see the dog and duck high up on the pub wall. The front part of the pub is a narrow space between the bar and the particularly fine Victorian mirrors on the party wall. The bar's unusual location against the wall rather than against the windows is delightfully eccentric.

Below: The back-to-front nature of The Dog & Duck's interior makes it an architectural gem as well as a notable Soho landmark.

THE DOVER CASTLE

ADDRESS: 43 WEYMOUTH MEWS, W1
BEERS: SAM SMITH'S OLD BREWERY BITTER
HOURS: MON–SAT 11.30AM–11PM

Nearby Portland Place was the grandest street in London in the 18th century. Laid out by Robert and James Adam around 1778, its exceptional width was the result of an order given by Lord Foley that the view northwards from the windows of his house – now the Langham Hotel – should not be obscured.

The street has an illustrious history. It is home to the headquarters of the BBC, several embassies, the Medical Research Council and the Royal Institute of British Architects. Lord Byron courted Anne Isabella Milbanke at No. 63, author John Buchan lived at No. 76 between 1912 and 1919, and from 1863 to 1866 No. 98 was the American Embassy; historian Henry Brooks Adams lived at the embassy while working for his father Charles Adams, Abraham Lincoln's ambassador to the Court of St James.

Considering this heritage, it is no surprise to learn that there are no pubs on Portland Place. So, if you have just been to a radio recording at Broadcasting House or enjoyed a stroll in Regent's Park and need refreshment, The Dover Castle is the place to go. Named after the Roman castle above the port of Dover, it dates back to around 1750 and has been licensed since 1777. Its discrete location behind the grand houses accounts for a less lavish interior compared with its near neighbour The Cock (see page 23).

The fact that the well-to-do did not want pubs as neighbours did not mean that they did not need their services. This is demonstrated on the front of The Dover Castle where, instead of the normal descriptions of 'public' and 'saloon', the doors are inscribed 'retail' and 'bottle', indicating that at one door the customers could come in and sit down for refreshment as usual, while at the other they would be served beers and wines to be taken away to supply the needs of the great houses. Today it is a luncheon pub popular with BBC staff, architects and doctors from the surrounding institutions, who can enjoy a reasonably priced meal in a variety of settings, given the various snugs and rooms.

Famous clientele include musicians such as The Who, who used it as a watering hole between sessions at the recording studios that stand opposite the pub.

Below: This 18th-century mews pub just off Portland Place is a lunchtime favourite with those in the know.

THE FITZROY TAVERN

◆

ADDRESS: 16 CHARLOTTE STREET, W1
BEERS: SAM SMITH'S OLD BREWERY BITTER
HOURS: MON–SAT 11.30AM–11PM; SUN 12 NOON–10.30PM

In 2001 an exhibition at the Museum of London traced the rise and fall of various artists' communities across London, from Covent Garden in the 17th century to present-day Hoxton. It demonstrated how every generation has thrown up a new set, with new ideas, in a new part of town. Longest lived and best known of these enclaves is Fitzrovia, which took its name from a truly Bohemian pub, The Fitzroy. Fitzrovia is the area between Oxford Street and Euston Road to the south and north, and Great Portland Street and Gower Street to the west and east.

The heart of Fitzrovia, Charlotte Street, was built in 1787 and named after the hugely popular wife of the hugely unpopular King George III. The street was an artists' quarter from the late 18th century to the 1950s. George Morland, an occasional lodger at The Fitzroy in 1776, can be considered Fitzrovia's first 'member'. Augustus John, who has a wall of the pub dedicated to him, was the last, dying in 1961. Other Fitzroy inhabitants included Dylan Thomas, artists' model Nina Hamnett ('Queen of Bohemia') and Tom Driberg, who in 1940 first coined the term 'Fitzrovia'.

The story of The Fitzroy is emblazoned on the walls, so there is no need to retell it here other than to point out that it is the story of a pub made great by the personality of a particular landlord. Indeed, truly great pubs are made by powerful personalities. In the case of The Fitzroy the hero of the piece was Judah 'Pop' Kleinfeld, who took over the pub in 1919 and whose genial face can be seen in photos there today. He passed the pub to his daughter Annie, and she and her husband Charles – a man with 'mine host' features if ever there was one – ran the pub until 1956. By the 1950s The Fitzroy's spreading fame was attracting tourist trade, which gradually drove the remaining Bohemians away to a new part of town that was suitably down at heel – Soho, and with it The French House (see pages 28–29) and the Colony Room.

Above: The Fitzroy Tavern's popularity among famous Bohemians in years past has resulted in the whole neighbourhood – Fitzrovia – taking its name.

The pub has lost a lot of the artefacts that helped make it such a great house, but there are still plenty of prints and pictures of The Fitzroy of yesteryear to create a vivid impression of what the pub was like in its heyday. Not to be missed is the downstairs bar with many pictures of former Fitzroy faces. Today it remains a hugely atmospheric pub.

THE FRENCH HOUSE

ADDRESS: 49 DEAN STREET, W1
BEERS: NO REAL ALES
HOURS: MON–SAT 12 NOON–11PM; SUN 12 NOON–10.30PM

The French House came into its own when Soho took over from Fitzrovia as the 'Bohemian' quarter of London, as The Fitzroy Tavern (see page 27) became a tourist attraction and as Soho's jazz scene started to take off. Dylan Thomas and Nina Hamnett were among those who migrated from The Fitzroy to The French House, and drinking buddies they picked up along the way included, among many others, Irish poet and playwright Brendan Behan and artist Francis Bacon.

The French House – or The French as regulars refer to it – was originally German. It was owned by a wine-shipper named Schmitt who ran it under its original name, the York Minster. In 1914 being German in London was bad for business, so the pub passed into the hands of Victor Berlemont, a colourful Belgian chef who had worked next door in the kitchens of the great Auguste Escoffier.

Maison Berlemont was a huge success, and its reputation drew international celebrities through the doors. Its fame was

so widespread that during the Second World War, French speakers fleeing Hitler and craving the comfort of something familiar chose to become regulars. It became a haunt of Free French officers, and it was here that Charles de Gaulle wrote his famous rejection of the Vichy settlement: 'La France a perdu une bataille. Mais la France n'a pas perdu la guerre!' ('France has lost a battle, but France hasn't lost the war!'). On D-Day, Soho, as home to a French community for 200 years, went wild and The French House was again the centre of attention.

With the end of the war a new phase in the life of The French took place. It is said that when Victor's son, Gaston, returned from the war and walked into the pub with uniform and kit bag, Victor said, 'Oh, you're back,' gave him the keys, put his hat on and left him to it. Gaston did his father proud, and maintained The French's character and reputation. Sporting a huge moustache like his father's, Gaston became one of Soho's celebrities, noted for his generosity and charity towards his more hard-up regulars: he advanced cash to some fairly famous folk.

Gaston locked up for the last time on Bastille Day, 14 July 1989, and the pub fortunately passed into the hands of French House regulars who wanted to keep the spirit alive. Apart from a few updating alterations and an official name change from the York Minster to The French House, the pub remains much as Victor and Gaston would have remembered it. It is so full of history and character that it has had an entire book dedicated to it; ask behind the bar for a copy – it's a cracking read.

Below left and below: The famous French House is one of those few pubs that only serves beer in half pints, and is principally a wine drinkers' venue.

THE GUINEA

◆

ADDRESS: 30 BRUTON PLACE, W1
BEERS: YOUNG'S BITTER, YOUNG'S SPECIAL, YOUNG'S TRIPLE A
HOURS: MON–FRI 10.30AM–11PM; SAT 6.30PM–11PM

Mayfair, which takes its name from a cattle market launched by James II in 1686, is now one of London's most exclusive areas. The cattle fair was suppressed in 1730, following increasing pressure to develop on the local land. It is likely that The Guinea dates from the time of this development.

The Guinea, sometimes referred to as the 'One Pound One' (a guinea being worth £1 and one shilling in old money), was one of London's first and finest mews pubs. The pub is no longer in a mews, however, North Bruton Mews having been renamed Bruton Place in line with the area's redevelopment in the 1930s. Fortunately, the 18th-century pub survived these changes and stands alone as a piece of local history.

The pub was first referred to as The Guinea in 1755, though previous incarnations of the establishment may have included The Running Horses, The Duke's Head or The Duke of Cumberland. Dating mainly from the early 19th century, the pub passed into the Young's estate in 1888. A restaurant was added in 1953, which built such a reputation for its steaks that it earned a celebrity clientele that included Princess Margaret, Richard Burton and Elizabeth Taylor, Charlton Heston, Jack Nicklaus and Frank Sinatra. It remains a popular choice among American visitors.

The pub itself is designed to cater for the peak-time, stand-up trade, being rather spartan with a tiny snug bar to one side. Nicotine-stained walls, dark wood surfaces and subdued lighting give the place a diffuse glow, and contribute to the pub's atmosphere of calm and egalitarian camaraderie in contrast to the reality of Mayfair outside.

Above: The Guinea is some 300 years old, in which time it has seen its locality undergo immense changes in character. By the 1950s The Guinea was London's first 'glitterati pub', with its restaurant attracting the rich and famous. The pub is now particularly well known for its award-winning steak-and-kidney pies.

HAND & RACQUET

◆

ADDRESS: 48 WHITCOMB STREET, WC2
BEERS: COURAGE BEST
HOURS: MON–SAT 11.30AM–11PM; SUN 12 NOON–10.30PM

At the southern extremities of Theatreland, or the West End, the theatres tend to be associated with comedy. Panton Street is home to the Comedy Theatre, while the Whitehall Theatre gave its name to a whole genre of farce. Between these two establishments lies the Hand & Racquet, which is itself not without comic connections. Situated on Whitcomb Street (which takes its name from a brewer, William Whitcomb, who started developing the area around the 1670s), the pub's name commemorates the tennis courts that formerly stood nearby. The pub's survival has contributed to the narrowness of Orange Street, on whose corner it sits, preventing the street from becoming a major thoroughfare. This in turn has contributed to the character of the pub, making it one of those hidden gems that allows drinkers to enjoy the delights of Leicester Square without putting up with its permanent crush.

Comedy is not confined to the nearby theatres either. Leicester Square is home to the original Comedy Store, which was the launch pad for many successful careers. A shortlist would have to include Rik Mayall, Adrian Edmondson, Jennifer Saunders, Dawn French, Keith Allen, Nigel Planer, Arthur Smith, Julian Clary, Harry Enfield, Rob Newman, David Baddiel, Jack Dee, Mark Lamar, Eddie Izzard, Tony Slattery, Steve Coogan, Jo Brand, Lee Evans, Sean Hughes, Frank Skinner and Lee Hurst. International names who have played there include Mike Myers, Ruby Wax, Emo Phillips, Dennis Leary and Robin Williams.

All these famous comics would, however, doff their caps to the Hand & Racquet, for the pub's comedy credentials are second to none. The legendary writing duo of Galton and Simpson, creators of *Hancock's Half Hour* and *Steptoe & Son* were frequent patrons. Unsurprisingly therefore, so too were Tony Hancock, his 'Carry On' sidekick Sid James, as well as the bumbling magician Tommy Cooper, whose televised death on the stage of Her Majesty's Theatre on 15 April 1984, just round the corner on Haymarket, stunned the nation.

Below: As the original comedy pub the Hand & Racquet has a distinguished list of former patrons, and it is still a haven from the area's crowds.

THE LAMB

ADDRESS: 94 LAMB'S CONDUIT STREET, WC1
BEERS: YOUNG'S BITTER, YOUNG'S SPECIAL, YOUNG'S TRIPLE A
HOURS: MON–SAT 12 NOON–11PM; SUN 12 NOON–3PM, 7PM–10.30PM

The trouble with forcing traffic into an organically evolved place like London is that, by enabling travel at a faster speed than the streets were intended to allow, the fabric of the city is distorted. In the late 19th century it was noted that the operation of a new omnibus service frequently destroyed many of the businesses along its route. Pubs were particularly vulnerable. The damage having been done, the 21st-century traveller is still conducted down thoroughfares and directed away from the side streets and byways where, by allowing people only to travel at the city's natural pace, the best of the city manages to survive.

Take, for example, The Lamb, probably the jewel in the crown of the Young's estate. Both The Lamb and the semi-pedestrianized street it sits upon are named after Sir William Lamb, a gentleman of the Chapel Royal under Henry VIII. In 1577 he improved an existing conduit to bring cleaner water down to the area from Holborn as an act of charity to benefit the neighbourhood. In addition he also donated 120 pails with which to carry the water from the conduit to the surrounding houses.

The pub itself was built in 1729, and though since remodelled, it is unusual in that many Victorian features remain – in particular one of the finest sets of snob screens to be found anywhere. These screens, dating from the 1870s, were a

Above: The Lamb has the flower baskets and well-maintained look that are characteristic of all Young's pubs and sits at the top of the steadily up-and-coming Lamb's Conduit Street.

fairly short-lived innovation. Small panels of opaque glass mounted at head height swivelled to allow the drinkers to place an order but remain anonymous to the rest of the pub. The pub would have been sub-divided into three or four partitions by panels that would have run from the bar to the walls. There are still clues to indicate where the panel partitions would have been. Snob screens were a product of Victorian street life, double standards and class distinction. People of different classes had to rub along together, but were very anxious that their behaviour should not be spied upon and commented on by their inferiors or superiors.

The pub also boasts an impressive collection of pictures of music-hall stars from the 1890s, all of whom performed at the now-demolished Holborn Empire. Reminiscent of those days, the pub even sports a working Polyphon, a very rare item. It is likely that Charles Dickens would have visited The Lamb while resident at nearby Doughty Street, where there is now a Dickens Museum. The British Museum is only a few minutes away.

Left: The Victorian bar is well worth a thorough examination for the quality of its architectural details.

LAMB AND FLAG

◆

ADDRESS: 33 ROSE STREET, WC2
BEERS: COURAGE BEST, CHARLES WELLS BOMBARDIER, MARSTON'S PEDIGREE
HOURS: MON–THURS 11AM–11PM; FRI–SAT 11AM–10.45PM; SUN 12 NOON–10.30PM

'Meum et propositum in taberna mori vinum. Sit appositum marlentis ori, ut decunt cum venerint angelorum chori. "Deus sit propitus huic potentori".' Who could possibly disagree with such stirring sentiments as expressed on the beams of the Lamb and Flag? Perhaps you would be more inclined to concur if you knew what it meant: 'To die in a tavern is my definite plan, with my mouth to the tap as close as I can, that the angels would say, when singing began, "O Lord please show mercy to this boozy man".' A home to boozy men the Lamb has certainly been. Booze would appear to have fuddled the memories of those first associated with the pub, as there are conflicting claims within the building as to whether it was built in 1623, 1635 or 1638.

Taking its name from a tavern, Rose Street was built in 1623 and bore one of the earliest street signs, which simply stated, 'This is Rose St 1623' (according to some authorities) or 'Red Rose St 1623' (according to others). The area was known as a particularly unsavoury neighbourhood throughout the 17th and 18th centuries; the poet Samuel Butler (author of *Hudibras*, a famous satire on Puritans) lived and died in the area in 1680. Lazenby Court, the low passageway to the side of the pub, in which it is still possible to crack your head, was built in 1688, a few years after another poet, the rather better known John Dryden, the Poet Laureate, was attacked and beaten in Rose Street in 1679, on account of some satirical lines he had written about the mistress of Charles II, the Duchess of Portsmouth. Dryden was clearly rather unlucky, for only three months later, on 18 December 1679, he was again beaten up in Rose Street, this time on the instruction of the Earl of Rochester; and before you aver that Mr Dryden must have been a man of poor judgement, the offending lines on the latter occasion were written by someone else.

The present inn was built in 1772 and is one of only a few timber-framed buildings in central London, having survived the Great Fire of 1666, though the exterior is Georgian.

Above: *The Lamb and Flag is an extremely popular Covent Garden watering hole, so much so that its customers tend to spill outside in all but the very worst weather and long into the night.*

Originally known as the Cooper's Arms, it was renamed the Lamb and Flag in 1883, and for some unknown reason the inn's sign is identical to the emblem of the Middle Temple Inn of Court. At one time the pub was nicknamed the Bucket of Blood, not because of the numbers of passers-by misjudging the height of Lazenby Court, but because of the prizefighting that took place there (see also The Salisbury, page 43). Charles Dickens was a frequent patron, but then he seems to have got about quite a lot.

THE MARQUIS OF GRANBY

ADDRESS: 51 CHANDOS PLACE, WC2

BEERS: TIMOTHY TAYLOR'S LANDLORD, ADNAM'S BITTER, BLACK SHEEP BITTER

HOURS: MON–SAT 12 NOON–11PM; SUN 12 NOON–10.30PM

London has a lot of pubs called The Marquis of Granby, which seems a bit strange since it has few other pubs named after marquises, and a marquis ranks far below a duke or an earl. John Manners, Marquis of Granby (1724–1770) ensured his place in posterity through his courage, popularity and generosity. It was at the Battle of Minden in 1759 during the Seven Years War that he made his name. Leading from the front, he was exhorting his men to advance when he decided to seize the moment and set his horse at full gallop against the enemy lines. The suddenness of the movement caused him to not only win the battle but also to lose his wig, giving rise to the expression 'going at it bald headed'.

As a leader the Marquis of Granby commanded great affection among his soldiers, and when hostilities ceased he presented many of his non-commissioned officers with a bounty paid from his own pocket. Many used this windfall to set themselves up as publicans and duly expressed their gratitude on their inn signs. Indeed, these signs invariably depict the marquis as bare-headed and balding – and never with a wig; this particular Marquis of Granby is no exception.

A comfortable pub at the bottom end of Theatreland, it is one of the cosier hostelries in the area, which is worth knowing on busy weekends. The building dates only from the 1880s but is located in an historic part of town. The blacking warehouse where Charles Dickens worked while his father was in the Marshalsea debtors' prison (featured in *Little Dorrit*) was nearby. The pub's site was originally occupied by the Hole in the Wall tavern, which was an outlaw hideout in London. The famous highwayman Claude Duval was taken here when too drunk to put up a fight. Duval's folk-hero status – he had once interrupted a coach robbery in order to dance a quadrille with a beautiful lady while her husband looked on, and then returned three-quarters of the money he had just taken as payment for the dance – was insufficient to save him from the law. He was hanged on 21 January 1760 and interred in the actors' church in nearby Covent Garden. John Manners suffered no better a fate than Duval; attacked by political rivals, his health failed and, tragically, he died in poverty.

Below: Many pubs share the title of The Marquis of Granby thanks to the peer's philanthropy, but this one in Soho is probably the capital's finest.

NEWMAN ARMS

ADDRESS: 23 RATHBONE STREET, W1
BEERS: FULLER'S LONDON PRIDE, BASS
HOURS: MON–FRI 12 NOON–11PM

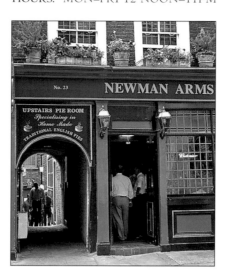

A pub is essentially a room, or perhaps two or three rooms, in which beer and other alcoholic beverages are sold. It is normally part of a larger building that contains the living quarters of the landlord, and it may or may not have upstairs function rooms, kitchens or gardens. From the customer's point of view it could all be just one room, as the skill of a publican lies in taking such a space and presenting it to the customer in such a way that they will do three things; enter, remain and return.

Built in 1760, the Newman Arms in Rathbone Street in Fitzrovia (See The Fitzroy Tavern, page 27) is an example of how this can be done. In essence the tiny pub is little more than a rectangle, broken up by the bar, which takes up two-thirds of the right side of the room. A tartan carpet manages, incredibly, not to clash with wallpaper of another tartan that covers those walls that aren't wood panelled. The prints that hang on the walls are all traditionally pub-like without reflecting a theme, and if there is a theme it must be taken from the clock bearing the legend 'Royal Navy Training College Dartmouth' in one corner and the model man-o'-war in a glass case on the other.

The pub retains its suitably authentic frontage, and a passage down the side – used in the Michael Powell film *Peeping Tom* (1960) – provides a handy entrance to the upstairs restaurant, known for its pies. The whole is a very small space, but the atmosphere is relaxed. The pub is not without its literary connections too, as George Orwell, before Fitzrovia existed for literary Londoners, used the pub twice: once in *Keep the Aspidistra Flying* and again in *Nineteen Eighty Four*.

Above and below: There are plenty of bigger and brasher pubs in the vicinity, but the diminutive nature of the Newman Arms only serves to improve the pub experience, which is both intimate and slightly surreal.

THE PORTERHOUSE

ADDRESS: 21–22 MAIDEN LANE, WC2
BEERS: PORTERHOUSE RANGE
HOURS: MON–SAT 11AM–11PM; SUN 12 NOON–10.30PM

One look in Maiden Lane will be sufficient for you to decide that the Porterhouse is not a traditional London pub. It is, however, a great London pub for the following reasons. In recent years in high-rent locations such as Covent Garden there has been a huge increase in competition for the money of Londoners and tourists alike. The 'superpub', i.e. one capable of absorbing around 500 people, is merely the latest manifestation in this on-going struggle, and Covent Garden and Leicester Square have seen an explosion in the number of superpubs. The majority of these establishments lack character and atmosphere; the exception is The Porterhouse.

This superpub works because of its is attention to detail and quality. The Porterhouse is vast, but deceptively so. It is

split into many levels, so you always feel you are in a rather smaller space than is actually the case. The varying levels are further broken up to create alcoves and intimate spaces. The usual decoration is case after case of bottled beer. There must be a couple of thousand bottles on display, and one does not need to be a beer aficionado to realize that this is a truly impressive global collection, reminiscent of the days when London pubs frequently did house huge collections of the weird and wonderful (see The Churchill Arms, page 117).

The next thing you quickly notice in this award-winning interior is the amount of copper. The contents of a small mine have been extracted and worked into banisters, chair backs, pipes, footrests and flues to create a warm glow throughout. There are even copper clocks and anglepoise lamps. Finally, the third thing one notices is The Porterhouse's own beers: they are all imported from the brewery of the same name in Dublin, and the beers are as diverse as they are carefully crafted. They are also totally unavailable elsewhere in London. A genuine Irish pub, therefore, so good *craic* is guaranteed.

Left: *Today the superpub is all too ubiquitous, but The Porterhouse is an example of how such transformations can be done successfully, and the result is truly impressive. One thing is sure: you will never be stuck for a tipple you fancy here.*

PRINCESS LOUISE

ADDRESS: 208 HIGH HOLBORN, WC1
BEERS: SAM SMITH'S OLD BREWERY BITTER
HOURS: MON–SAT 11AM–11PM; SUN 12 NOON–10.30PM

The philistines who ran Watney's Brewery so unsuccessfully that it is now no more than an unpleasant memory, once wanted to demolish the Princess Louise in order to build office blocks. This would have been an act of criminal proportions, but not an unusual one in the history of brewing in the 20th century.

The Princess Louise has one claim to fame, one reason why it is one of the absolute must-visit pubs in London: its interior. The Princess Louise retains the finest, most complete, most original, best preserved, most authentic high-Victorian pub interior in London. It is a national treasure. It is rumoured that even the gents' toilets – by J. Tylor & Sons of London & Sydney no less – are listed and, gentlemen, once you have paid them a visit other urinals will seem mean by comparison.

The spectacular thing about the Princess is the degree of craftsmanship displayed on almost every surface. What is often forgotten today is the extent to which our late great Victorian 'gin palace'-style pubs were not just opulent because opulence was the fashion, they were opulent because they could afford to be. To truly understand the Princess Louise, and the other great pub interiors of the time, you need to understand that they were also a statement of nationhood. The pub was built in 1872, named after a daughter of Queen Victoria, and was remodelled in 1891 to more or less its present form. It was very much a pub of its day, and its day was the height of the British Empire, when Britain was home to a very proud race who happened to be running the largest empire the world had ever seen. Britain was also the 'workshop of the world', its craftsmen were the best in the world, and the Victorians liked to be reminded of this. R. Morris Ltd

of 293 Kennington Road, south-east London, were so proud of the beautiful mirrors they produced for the Princess Louise that they signed them.

A glance at the rich lincrusta ceiling indicates that the pub was previously subdivided with a narrow corridor along the side – much like The Argyll Arms (see page 18) – and the comparison of these two pubs is a useful reminder that the Princess Louise was once unexceptional. Sadly, what the Luftwaffe did not destroy brewery accountants set out to. In many cases they were rather more successful than the Luftwaffe. The Princess survives as much by luck as by judgement, as what is a wonder to one generation can seem mundane to another – incredibly it does not warrant much mention in the pub guides of the 1960s, other than a passing note that it was a popular venue for folk music in the 1950s.

Above and below: The rather plain exterior of this pub gives little clue as to what is on offer inside. The Princess Louise boasts one of England's finest pub interiors and is a monument to 19th-century craftsmanship.

QUEENS LARDER

ADDRESS: I QUEEN SQUARE, WCI

BEERS: BASS, FULLER'S LONDON PRIDE, MARSTON'S PEDIGREE, BODDINGTONS

HOURS: MON–SAT IIAM–IIPM; SUN 12 NOON–10.30PM

The pub now known as the Queens Larder is known to have existed in 1720 as a humble alehouse without a sign. Later in the century, George III, who was to become the longest reigning monarch since Henry III, started to show signs of the mental illness with which the modern public is so familiar following the success of the play and film about him.

During the initial period of his illness, when news of his incapacity was too sensitive to be made public – and indeed the nature of his illness was not understood – the king was confined in Queen Square at the home of his physician Dr Willis. The king's wife, Queen Charlotte, rented a small cellar under the alehouse in which secretly to store delicacies and provisions that might relieve the tedium and misery of the king's confinement. Queen Square is not named after her, but after Queen Anne, who died in 1712 while the square was being built (1708–20); there is, however, a statue of Queen Charlotte in the square, although this has nothing to do with recognition of her compassion towards her husband, as it was erected between 1775 and 1780 and his first confinement was not until 1788–9.

George III had one further period of severe mental instability in 1801 and finally became deranged in 1810, occasioning his hugely unpopular and much less cultured son to act as Regent until the king's death in 1820. As a consequence of her devotion to her husband, the pub was renamed the Queens Larder once the facts of the matter had entered the public domain.

Queen Square has always been something of a centre for philanthropy and medicine. The Foundling Hospital was next to the square in Guildford Street, founded in 1742 by Captain Thomas Coram who was frequently appalled by the sight of small children exposed in the streets, abandoned by their parents and 'left to die in dung hills'. After 17 years' work among these children he persuaded 21 ladies of nobility and distinction to petition the king, and in 1739 a Royal Charter was granted for The Hospital for the Maintenance and Education of Exposed and Deserted Young Children. Coram numbered among his benefactors many of the great and good, who were enthused by the success of this remarkable institution. Hogarth helped provide decorations for the Court Room of the hospital, as did Gainsborough and Reynolds. In 1749 Handel wrote the *Foundling Hospital Anthem* as a fundraiser. The Great Ormond Street Hospital for Sick Children is also just off Queen Square.

Above and left: The Queens Larder is a reminder that our pubs and their names are all part of the nation's history. This pub serves a secluded and very attractive corner of the city and offers a lovely ambience.

THE RED LION

ADDRESS: CROWN PASSAGE, SW1
BEERS: COURAGE BEST, ADNAM'S BITTER
HOURS: MON–SAT 11AM–11PM

The Red Lion is one of London's great establishments. It is true that the clubs of Pall Mall, St James's Palace, Clarence House, and the exclusive shops on St James's Street are all grander, but whether they are more important is open to debate. For a start, without the customers of The Red Lion none of these other establishments could operate. The clientele comprises the chefs and doormen of the clubs, the hatters and wine merchants of St James, the royal protection officers from the palaces. It also comprises gentlemen popping in for a beer before moving on to stuffier surroundings, or the clients of the said hatters and wine merchants, and all the while The Red Lion is one of the most egalitarian and companionable pubs in London. There is a fair sprinkling of tourists, who have heard about it from other tourists with the words 'If you visit just one pub…'

If you were to list all the people who had popped into The Red Lion to pass an idle few minutes and had left hours later with a new band of lifelong friends it would run into the thousands. It is a totally magical and very happy place. At least 330 years old, it is the holder of the second oldest licence in London. It proudly claims to be London's oldest village inn, and if you climb upstairs to the small first-floor lounge you can experience the basis of this claim: it is absolutely charming and designed to make you forget you are in London.

In its heyday the pub was a 'wenching house', and recent restoration unearthed a mysterious glass panel set into a floor which could only have be used for voyeuristic purposes (which may also explain the early licence, as influential patrons often sought to safeguard their recreation). There are, allegedly, secret passages leading to St James's Palace, although this seems unlikely if you study the local geography. The pub is

certainly in what was one of the most rakish parts of London. The courtyard of nearby Berry Bros & Rudd wine merchants was the scene of London's last legal duel. The loser breathed his last on the floor of The Red Lion. More refined patrons have included actor Pierce Brosnan, who used the pub while filming scenes at the nearby Reform Club for the James Bond film *Die Another Day*.

Right: Beyond the obvious bucketfuls of character that The Red Lion owes to its location and age, it is also a great pub thanks to a wonderful relationship that exists between the customers and the bar staff.

THE RED LION

◆

ADDRESS: 2 DUKE OF YORK STREET, SW1
BEERS: TETLEY, ADNAM'S BITTER
HOURS: MON–FRI 11.30AM–11PM; SAT 12 NOON–11PM

Is there anything truly extraordinary about The Red Lion to earn it the accolade of being London's most photographed pub interior? If there is, no one really seems to know what it is. An obvious reason behind its fame is undoubtedly its magnificent decoration, but that is only part of the story, and the main reason for its fame is simply its survival. Without wishing to sound too glib, the reason why it has survived is that it has not been destroyed, and

it has not been destroyed because no one has managed to drop a bomb on it. Part of The Red Lion's appeal, therefore, is as a reminder of the hundreds of fine pubs that did not survive either the Blitz, road-widening initiatives, slum clearances or redevelopments.

The Red Lion was built, as its Georgian façade suggests, in 1821, on the site of an earlier pub, as was common, and it was remodelled in the 1870s, which was equally common. Evidence of the remodelling work can be found in the varying styles of glasswork, for which the pub is famous — that in the doors and partitions is earlier than that in the ornate mirrors. The mirrors, which may have been crafted by Walter Gibbs and Sons of Blackfriars, cover nearly every wall surface and are the product of later improvements in the techniques of engraving and etching. Some believe that the reason behind such an abundance of mirrors was an initiative by magistrates to reduce the privacy of the snugs and thereby reduce the chances of casual prostitution taking place in the pub.

The pub is small and this serves to remind us that in its heyday its clientele, though numerous, would probably only have been inclined, or able, to stay for shorter periods — popping in and out would have been the norm. The pub would nevertheless have been a bustling centre of activity and information, and a focus for the scandal and gossip emanating from the grand houses and clubs of St James.

Nearby attractions include the London Library, the Royal Academy, Fortnum and Mason's, and the shops of Jermyn Street. St James's Piccadilly, a church designed by Sir Christopher Wren and a popular concert venue, is only 20 yards away.

Left: Another great survivor, this Georgian Red Lion escaped the Blitz and as such is an excellent reminder of the style of pubs that would once have littered the streets of central London.

THE RED LION

ADDRESS: 48 PARLIAMENT STREET, SW1
BEERS: TETLEY, BASS, ADNAM'S BITTER
HOURS: MON–SAT 11AM–11PM; SUN 12 NOON–7PM

There is a lake in Wales into which, according to legend, a stream flows in and out without ever mixing with the waters of the lake. The Red Lion in Parliament Street is a bit like that. A constant stream of tourists pass through this narrow Westminster pub, never to return, while a dedicated band of regulars returns day in and day out. A third group consists of those who have finished their day's business in the Palace of Westminster, Downing Street or the Treasury, and wish to ponder the success or otherwise of their mission.

Anyone who falls into the latter two groups is likely to know the landlord Raoul de Vere, who is one of the trade's truly larger-than-life characters. A former policeman and now a magistrate, he is a pioneer of the Pubwatch scheme of pub/police co-operation and an industry figure whose opinion is frequently sought by legislators. The pub itself is directly opposite the Treasury building, which was designed by the impressive architectural trio of William Kent, Sir John Soane and Sir Charles Barry and completed in 1845.

The Red Lion is also a few doors down from the house of Sir George Burke, a friend of Isambard Kingdom Brunel, who lodged directly across the street. Brunel ran a piece of string attached to a bell across the street in order to summon his friend to the window so he could telegraph messages to him or beckon him to go for an early morning walk.

The pub sports a rather lopsided aspect – it is long and narrow and the bar runs along one wall beneath the stairs up to the dining room, which gained notoriety in the early 1990s as a place where Labour modernizers gathered to hatch New Labour. The pictures on the walls are very much of a political nature. When the metropolitan police were in Scotland Yard it was very much their pub. Charles Dickens was also familiar with The Red Lion – he used it as the inn where David Copperfield asked for 'a glass of Genuine Stunning' ale and was given it with a kiss; this has earned him a bust high up in the wall. Geoffrey Chaucer is also honoured with a bust, but since there has only been a pub on the site since 1437, it is impossible that he would ever have supped here.

Below: The politicians' pub, The Red Lion played a role in carving out the destiny of New Labour; and thanks to its location there is every reason to believe that political shenanigans go on there today.

THE RED LION

ADDRESS: 1 WAVERTON STREET, W1

BEERS: COURAGE BEST, COURAGE DIRECTORS, THEAKSTON'S XB, GREENE KING IPA

HOURS: MON–FRI 11.30AM–11PM; SAT 6PM–9.30PM; SUN 12 NOON–3PM, 6PM–9PM

A pub commentator of the early 1970s once maintained that there was a breed of London pub that could be termed 'The Mayfair Pub', and to prove his point he selected The Red Lion as the epitome of the style. It is, he said, 'one of Mayfair's most stylish and popular pubs with spacious bars, a good dining area, an excellent cold buffet counter and pleasing décor that includes several paintings both old and new'. The fine paintings have departed, presumably along with a previous landlord, but all else remains the same.

It is ironic that this Red Lion should be the epitome of a style, since the three other Red Lions in this book are each the epitome of the three elements that come together to make a great pub. The Red Lion in Crown Passage has a notable clientele, the one in Parliament Street has a notable landlord and that in Duke of York Street has a notable interior.

This Red Lion undoubtedly has a notable neighbourhood. Situated amid some of London's most expensive real estate, it would be surprising if this fact were not reflected in The Red Lion and, indeed, it exudes a certain casual gentility, from the leaded windows to the one-man settles and the artefacts arranged on shelves all around the wood-panelled bar. Built in the mid-18th century as a refreshment house for grooms and domestic servants, it has, like its 'mews'-style counterparts, been colonized by the well-to-do. Hence the rather fine restaurant to the rear. To the front is a small outdoor overspill area, which is a surprising suntrap on a hot summer's day.

Above and below: This Red Lion is a winner in every respect, perfect for a quiet drink outside or a hearty meal in cosy surroundings.

THE SALISBURY

ADDRESS: 90 ST MARTIN'S LANE, WC2
BEERS: COURAGE DIRECTORS, THREE GUEST ALES
HOURS: MON–SAT 11AM–11PM; SUN 12 NOON–10.30PM

One of central London's most spectacular pub interiors belongs to a pub with quite a history. At one time The Salisbury was known as the Coach & Horses, then it became the Ben Caunt's Head after a landlord who also enjoyed celebrity as a bare-knuckle fighter (aka the Nottinghamshire Giant). In the early 19th century it was well known as a venue for pugilistic contests, notably the return from retirement of Jim Belcher to face a challenge from 'the Game Chicken' – sadly, history does not record the result.

In 1892 a new lease was taken out on the property from the Marquis of Salisbury, a favourite of Queen Victoria and a direct descendant of Robert Cecil, the first Earl of Salisbury (a favourite of Queen Elizabeth I). The marquis was a good friend of public houses too. When Temperance campaigners argued that a reduction in the number of pubs would lead to a reduction in drunkenness his lordship replied that he could not follow the logic of their argument; after all, he said, he owned an awful lot of bedrooms but he did not find that that led to him sleeping more. The pub was already known as The Salisbury Stores, which would indicate that it acted as a wine merchant's as well as a gin palace.

The pub was rebuilt in 1898, and it is this magnificent interior that we are fortunate enough to enjoy today; although the pub was restored in 1963, it was done in the most sympathetic manner. Being located in the heart of Theatreland the pub has enjoyed a great many theatrical connections. In the days when homosexuality was a criminal offence, it was something of a haven for London's theatrical gay community. In the 1960s, when 'Stores' was dropped from its name, it enjoyed a vogue as 'the actors' pub'. These days it is more likely to be full of audiences rather than actors, now that the days of celebrity worship and paparazzi make a relaxed drink impossible for stars. The pub was famously used as a location in the 1961 Dirk Bogarde movie *The Victim*.

The Salisbury is ideally situated for refreshment before or after engaging in a wide variety of nearby entertainment. There is opera to be had at the Coliseum and candlelit concerts at St Martin-in-the-Fields. Famous faces are to be seen at the National Portrait Gallery and the brushstrokes of old masters can be examined in the National Gallery. And, of course, there are always the theatres.

Above and below: The Salisbury boasts one of the most flamboyant and high-Victorian interiors of all London pubs, which perhaps explains its popularity with a flamboyant clientele.

THE SEVEN STARS

ADDRESS: 53 CAREY STREET, WC2

BEERS: HARVEY'S SUSSEX BITTER, ADNAM'S BITTER, ADNAM'S BROADSIDE, ADNAM'S REGATTA

HOURS: MON–FRI 11AM–11PM; SAT 12 NOON–11PM

The Seven Stars is an outpost of Soho and a city institution in its own right. The pub is said to have been built in 1602 and survived the Great Fire of London of 1666, though how much of the present fabric of the building is original is open to debate. Nevertheless, a rustic feel pervades this simple pub, both inside and out.

It is reported to have originally been named the League of Seven Stars after the seven provinces that make up the Netherlands, on account of the fact that Dutch sailors were reputed to have settled in the neighbourhood. If the Dutch did have a presence here they have left precious little sign of it elsewhere in the vicinity. Also departed from the neighbourhood, and very nearly forgotten, are the bankruptcy courts, from the days when bankruptcy was an offence and bankrupts – such as Charles Dickens's father – would find themselves in debtors' prisons such as the Marshalsea in Southwark (Dickens set *Little Dorritt* around the Marshalsea and was familiar with The Seven Stars). To be in Carey Street, the street on which the pub stands, was once a London euphemism for being 'brassic', 'skint' or 'broke' – all good London terms, too.

Today the pub is entirely surrounded by London's legal community. The rear of the Royal Courts of Justice provides the view from the pub doorway, while Lincoln's Inn, one of the four Inns of Court, is to the rear. They are referred to as 'inns' in the same way that a pub may be an inn, as they both derive from the old English word for a chamber. One attraction of this visually striking pub is the landlady, the exotically named Roxy Beaujolais. A quick perusal of the walls will enable you to ascertain that she is very much a figure in the London pub scene, and astute readers may be able to work out who she is sitting next to in the photo captioned 'Three Greyhounds 1996'.

Those fortunate enough not to have business at either the Royal Courts of Justice or Lincoln's Inn might have time to visit the Soane Museum on the north side of Lincoln's Inn Fields, the former house of the famous architect Sir John Soane, designer of the Dulwich Picture Gallery (see The Crown & Greyhound, page 142). Alternatively, you could walk through Lincoln's Inn to Chancery Lane and the London Silver Vaults, one of London's great hidden treasures – literally.

Above and left: The Seven Stars presents a very conservative frontage to Carey Street; inside, political humour dating back to the battles between Whigs and Tories sits side by side with film posters on the walls of this perennially busy pub.

THE SHERLOCK HOLMES

ADDRESS: 10–11 NORTHUMBERLAND STREET, WC2
BEERS: BASS, BODDINGTONS, FLOWERS, MORLAND'S OLD SPECKLED HEN
HOURS: MON–SAT 11AM–11PM; SUN 12 NOON–10.30PM

You are as unlikely to find a local inside The Sherlock Holmes as you are a Parisian up the Eiffel Tower, but the fact that it is an unashamed tourist trap does not mean that it is not worth a visit. The pub has an incredible charm, and this is down to a single-minded and very theatrical devotion to its subject, Sherlock Holmes. Holmes covers just about every possible surface. Three-dimensional artefacts are just as common as two-dimensional prints, and the whole, surrounding the central ground-floor bar, creates a very Victorian feel that the great sleuth himself would probably have felt comfortable with... if he had ever existed that is – though you might be forgiven for thinking that he actually had, for there are precious few references to his creator, Sir Arthur Conan Doyle.

Much of the Holmes collection was acquired as a job lot in 1957 from the winding up of the 1951 Festival of Britain's world tour, and a pub seemed the obvious home for such a collection. Whitbread selected the Northumberland Arms as home for the Holmes hoard. Conan Doyle would, like as not, have approved of the choice of venue for it is next door to the Northumberland Hotel, London retreat of his character Sir Henry Baskerville. The chief attraction is Holmes's study on one side of the main restaurant, set up much as it was displayed round the world in the 1950s.

Continuing interest in Sherlock Holmes, one of Britain's most popular literary exports, ensures that the collection keeps expanding. Each new film and television series provides further material for the archives, making The Sherlock Holmes as much an attraction as a place to go between attractions. Having said that, it is excellently situated for a whole number of London sights: Trafalgar

Above: It may be unashamedly tacky and a very popular refreshment stop with tourists, but there is no doubting that an awful lot of fun is to be had in The Sherlock Holmes.

Square, the National Portrait Gallery, St James's Park, Buckingham Palace, the London Eye and the South Bank are all within easy walk.

THE SHIP & SHOVELL

ADDRESS: 1–3 CRAVEN PASSAGE, WC2
BEERS: BADGER BEST BITTER, TANGLEFOOT, KING AND BARNES SUSSEX
HOURS: MON–FRI 11AM–11PM; SAT 12 NOON–11PM

The novelist and writer on London Peter Ackroyd likes to think of London as a living organism, an entity with a spirit brought to life by 2,000 years of human activity on one spot. In the oldest parts of London, as in Ackroyd's beloved Clerkenwell, that spirit is almost tangible; there are eddies and currents in the city that defy the zeitgeist. Starbucks and McDonalds may shape the look of modern London, but away from the homogenized high streets lies the old city, shaped by the deep, subliminal nature of Londoners.

Take, for example, The Ship & Shovell. Located just behind Charing Cross Station and the Embankment, it is a few tantalizing paces from thronging Villiers Street, yet is a mystery to all but a handful of the thousands of scurrying figures who daily pass within 50 yards of it. The pub was established around 1740, but sadly lay derelict between 1981 and 1996, when it was renovated and restored by the present owners. They tired of the view opposite, which was of another derelict property, and took it over, connected the two beneath the pavement of Crown Passage and opened it as a half-pub in 1999. It is now unique as the only pub with two frontages facing each other.

The lateral thinking powers of the licensees do not end there. They realized that the pub lacked a certain Christmas cheer as a huge number of their customers are commuters who are totally absent at Christmas. Accordingly, the pub celebrates Christmas when its customers are around, in June as it happens, complete with tree and Christmas raffle. It only needs another hundred years for people to forget the origins of the practice to make it yet another truly great London tradition.

The pub takes its name from Admiral Sir Cloudesley Shovell (1650–1707) who, like Nelson, joined the navy at the age of 13, rising to earn a commission — an exceptional feat at a time when most were purchased. Prior to his appointment as Admiral of the Fleet, he lived at nearby May Place. His career highlight came with the capture of Gibraltar and his promotion to Commander in Chief of the English Fleet. Sadly, this exalted position was his downfall, for in 1707 his flagship, HMS *Association*, foundered off the Scilly Isles and, as he struggled ashore, he was strangled by a local woman desperate to steal his emerald ring.

Above and below: Laterally thinking landlords have made The Ship & Shovell a rising star among London pubs in recent years; or should that be The Ship & Shovells? This unique pub has two frontages facing each other across a narrow backstreet.

STAR & GARTER

ADDRESS: 62 POLAND STREET, W1
BEERS: FULLER'S LONDON PRIDE, COURAGE BEST
HOURS: MON–SUN 11AM–11PM

The Star & Garter has had the very good fortune of having been left well alone by modern tastes, and the result is a Soho pub that is not trying to make a statement, or trying too hard to attract a certain crowd. Appearing in Poland Street as the Star & Garter in around 1825, the pub takes its name from the badge of the Order of the Garter, one of the highest remaining chivalric orders in the United Kingdom, along with the Order of the Bath.

A fine mirror bearing the star and garter forms the focus of the pub. The garter bears the motto of the British monarchy, which dates back to the days of Edward III, who in 1348 first uttered the words 'Honi soit qui mal y pense' – 'Evil be to he that thinks it'. According to legend, at a ball, possibly held at Calais, Joan Countess of Salisbury dropped her garter and King Edward, seeing her embarrassment, picked it up and bound it about his own leg saying in French, 'Evil (or shamed) be he that thinks evil of it'; however, this is almost certainly a later fiction. It is much more likely that the device was a small strap, possibly used to attach pieces of armour, and was used as a symbol of binding together in common brotherhood; the motto probably refers to the leading political topic of the 1340s, Edward's claim to the throne of France.

Poland Street began life in the 1680s and building continued until about 1707. It takes its name from a pub originally called the King of Poland, which was known as the Dickens Wine House when it was destroyed by a bomb in 1940. The street's most famous resident was William Blake, who lends his name to the Star & Garter's upstairs bar. Blake lived at No. 28 from 1785 to 1791, and was a neighbour of Elizabeth Billington, who, being the mistress of both the Duke of Rutland and the Prince of Wales, must have been quite a beauty. Those being the days when everyone in London knew everyone's business, she was disapprovingly known as the 'Poland Street Man Trap'.

Below: A no-frills, honest-to-goodness local right in the heart of Soho, which makes a welcome reprieve from the showiness that often dominates the area.

The City & The East End

Many pubs in London are great survivors, and none more so than those of the City and the East End, where whole swaths of land were left desolate by the Blitz and then depersonalized by post-war developments. In recent years, there has been something of a revival of these areas and their communities, and as a result more people are discovering the great pubs that have shaped the character of the area through hard times and good times. Whatever your mood, you'll find a pub to please, as there is everything here, from traditional East End boozers, such as The Pride of Spitalfields, to the jaw-dropping elaborate décor of The Black Friar, to secluded establishments such as Ye Olde Mitre Tavern.

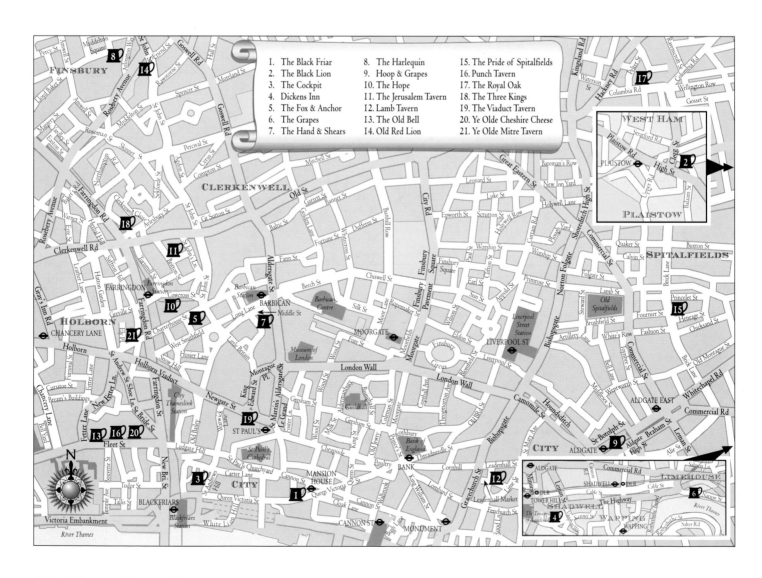

1. The Black Friar
2. The Black Lion
3. The Cockpit
4. Dickens Inn
5. The Fox & Anchor
6. The Grapes
7. The Hand & Shears
8. The Harlequin
9. Hoop & Grapes
10. The Hope
11. The Jerusalem Tavern
12. Lamb Tavern
13. The Old Bell
14. Old Red Lion
15. The Pride of Spitalfields
16. Punch Tavern
17. The Royal Oak
18. The Three Kings
19. The Viaduct Tavern
20. Ye Olde Cheshire Cheese
21. Ye Olde Mitre Tavern

THE BLACK FRIAR

ADDRESS: 174 QUEEN VICTORIA STREET, EC4
BEERS: ADNAM'S BITTER, FULLER'S LONDON PRIDE, TIMOTHY TAYLOR'S LANDLORD
HOURS: MON–FRI 11.30AM–11PM

The staggering fact one learns on a visit to The Black Friar is that it was due for demolition in the 1960s. Today it is a Grade I listed building, but it took a public outcry to save this unique pub from the wrecker's ball. The Black Friar holds a special place of affection in Londoners' hearts – it is so completely over the top that you cannot but fall in love with it. There is something naughty about the images of rotund, jovial friars, seemingly neglecting their devotions in favour of more worldly pleasures, that appeals to the London psyche. A Dominican friary stood on the site from 1279 to the Reformation in 1539, and the black-habited order lent its name to the area as well as the pub.

It is amazing that the pub exists at all: it was built in 1902–04 in an Anglicized Art Nouveau style at a time when the London pub market had crashed and bankruptcies were many times more common than new building works.

Consequently, there are very few London pubs dating from this era (see also The Coal Hole, page 22), and those that survive are wonderfully idiosyncratic. The narrow end of the building assumes a mock baronial hall style, which gives over to a sumptuous and intimate room at the back that defies analogy. Friezes in copper and plaster by Henry Poole RA depicting monks having a good time hover above signs offering such pearls of wisdom as 'finery is foolery', or 'don't advertise, tell a gossip'. There are upwards of 50 different types of marble employed in the building, which, with authentic Art Nouveau light fittings, furniture and wood carving lends the whole an air that – a preponderance of cowls and habits notwithstanding – tempts one to feel rather indulgent.

The sign over the slight partition between the two parts of the bar suggests that this site was where the Holy Roman Emperor Charles V, the Papal Magistrate and Henry VIII all met in 1532 to discuss the dissolution of Henry's marriage to Catherine of Aragon. It is not hard to imagine the bluff King Henry propping up the bar, though no doubt the sight of him would wipe the smiles from the faces of the jolly monks.

Below: London's only true Art Nouveau public house, The Black Friar is unique for its elaborate interior, and is all the more surprising for having been built during a slump in pub property prices.

Previous page: As its name suggests, The Cockpit was once the scene of many a cockfight before the practice was banned in 1849.

THE BLACK LION

ADDRESS: PLAISTOW HIGH STREET, E13
BEERS: COURAGE BEST AND COURAGE DIRECTORS
HOURS: MON–WED 11AM–3PM, 5PM–11PM; THUR–SAT 11AM–11PM; SUN 12 NOON–10.30PM

Originally built over 600 years ago, The Black Lion was reconstructed about 280 years ago. Many features of the early coaching inn remain, such as the cobbled coaching yard. The pub is extensive, and is a good example of how we have forgotten about many of the ancillary functions that such houses used to provide and which required a depth of property much greater than just a front bar, which is all that so many of us see in a pub today. Go through to the coaching yard, which is defended by a stout oak gate, and you will see the old stables area, now converted into kitchen space. Part of the former coaching yard is now a beer garden.

The Black Lion is one of only a few London pubs that still retain a boxing association. The West Ham Boys Boxing Club trains in a hall to the left of the courtyard; it has a fine pedigree of graduates too. It was home to Terry Spinks, the first Briton to win an Olympic boxing gold, at the 1956 Games; George Walker, creator of the Brent Walker pubs and clubs empire, trained here with his brother Billy; while champion prize-fighters Barry McGuigan and Nigel Benn have both worked out at The Black Lion. Sporting connections do not end with boxing, for the pub was popular with West Ham footballers, and the 1966 World Cup England captain, Bobby Moore, was a regular.

Inside the pub you are transported into the countryside. Low ceilings, wood floors, oak beams, bare brick walls adorned with brewery ephemera acquired over generations all give the impression of a rural inn rather than a town pub. Several generations are also well represented here. There have been only six landlords since 1929, and Milly Morris, a famous East End barmaid, served behind the bar from 1929 until 1997. She was able to regale customers with tales about the pub during the Second World War when the cellars were used as air-raid shelters. Evidence of the shelters is still to be seen, although no longer visible are the smugglers' tunnels which extend over half a mile to emerge very close to the Upton Park football ground, and with which the notorious highwayman Dick Turpin may well have been familiar – for he used to stable Black Bess in what is now the function room.

Below: Everyone from legendary highwayman Dick Turpin to the footballing legend Bobby Moore has drunk at this down-to-earth East End pub.

THE COCKPIT

ADDRESS: 7 ST ANDREWS HILL, EC4
BEERS: COURAGE BEST, COURAGE DIRECTORS, MARSTON'S PEDIGREE
HOURS: MON–FRI 11AM–11PM; SAT 11AM–7PM; SUN 12 NOON–7PM

The Cockpit is a bit out of place in EC4, as it looks much more like an East End boozer than a City one; but this is its charm – it even opens on a Sunday. Dating from the 16th century, it may well have been familiar to William Shakespeare. It was originally known as The Cock Pit (as two words), and cockfighting was one of its main activities and attractions. When cockfighting was banned in 1849 the pub's name changed to The Three Castles (one of which would have been for Baynard's Castle, a Norman fortress that stood at the foot of St Andrew's Hill until the Great Fire of 1666). Refurbishment of the pub in the 1970s saw the introduction of a spectators' gallery around the first-floor interior and the restoration of The Cockpit name.

The Cockpit is also the proud owner of a rare shove-ha'penny board – ask behind the bar for the necessary old pennies, and there will be no shortage of willing locals offering to show you how to play.

Just as the 2,000 year-old City is ever changing, The Cockpit reminds you that there are aspects of it that stay remarkably constant. The Londoner is one of these, and The Cockpit is a Londoner's pub. Many customers today will be direct descendants of those who went to watch the bird fights in centuries past, and are drawn from the invisible City – the one that does not draw large salaries or award itself fat bonuses,

but provides all the services and necessities for the one that does.

This is why the pub opens on a Sunday, because many of its customers have to work on Sunday too. For this reason it is popular with the bell ringers of St Paul's Cathedral; it is also open on Good Friday. If you should find yourself in the City on a Sunday, which will be more likely now that the Millennium Bridge is open to ferry people from the Tate Modern to St Paul's Cathedral, it is worth remembering that The Cockpit is probably the only pub you will find open between the Embankment and Liverpool Street.

Above and below: The traditional Victorian exterior of The Cockpit does not reflect its mock-Tudor interior. Honest the décor may not be, but this is a true East End pub sat within the City walls and a reminder of the community that has been here since long before the City became a financial centre.

DICKENS INN

◆

ADDRESS: ST KATHARINE'S DOCK, E1
BEERS: COURAGE BEST, COURAGE DIRECTORS, MORLAND'S OLD SPECKLED HEN, THEAKSTON'S OLD PECULIER
HOURS: MON–SAT 11AM–11PM; SUN 12 NOON–10.30PM

Dickens Inn was originally a brewery building dating from the 18th century that was later used as a spice warehouse. Then, some 25 years ago, it was painstakingly relocated, timber by timber, to the exclusive St Katharine's Dock. For those with an interest in construction, photographs of the meticulous process are on display in the pub. Despite its age, fans of Charles Dickens should note that, beyond its new location, there is no connection between the building, the pub or the prolific novelist.

St Katharine's Dock itself opened in 1828, having been designed and built in an impressively speedy two years by the engineer Thomas Telford of canal- and bridge-building fame to create extra capacity for London's overstretched port space. The spoil from the excavations was carted off to Belgrave Square (see The Star Tavern, page 88), and the resultant dock specialized in cargoes such as ivory and spices. Bomb damage in the last war ended St Katharine's commercial history. It fell into disuse, and the local pubs also suffered as London's port trade contracted to the Isle of Dogs and the Royal Docks.

The docks' warehouses have since been converted into luxury apartments and shops, and many fine yachts of the rich and famous can be spotted in the marina.

Dickens Inn opened in 1976 in 'the style of a 19th century balconied two storied inn' (sic), despite the fact that according to the history books there never was such a thing and that it is actually three storeys. The timber construction makes it one of the more unusual pubs in London, and it is a large, loud and fun place to drink. Each floor offers something different in the way of food, becoming more expensive as you climb up the stairs – bar food, pizza restaurant and finally an expensive restaurant on the top floor. Dickens Inn is a good place to start or finish a riverside walk or from which to enjoy the Tower of London and the many attractions south of Tower Bridge.

Left: The tranquil surroundings of St Katharine's Dock make The Dickens Inn a good place to refresh along the riverside.

THE FOX & ANCHOR

ADDRESS: 115 CHARTERHOUSE STREET, EC1
BEERS: ADNAM'S BITTER, FULLER'S LONDON PRIDE
HOURS: MON–THURS 7AM–3PM; FRI 7AM–9.30PM

Tucked into Charterhouse Street in one of the very oldest parts of London, The Fox & Anchor enjoys that supreme imprimatur of excellence that can be only gained and never awarded – recognition. Mention The Fox & Anchor to a Londoner and they will know you are referring to breakfast. Gluttons should be able to compare the relative merits of the breakfast at The Fox & Anchor and The Hope (see page 61) in the same morning, as they are only a matter of some 100 yards apart. Both establishments have a special licence that allows them to open early and serve breakfast and beer to workers at the nearby Smithfield Market, and naturally they pride themselves on the excellence and freshness of their meat.

The Fox is a handsome specimen, and was the winner of the English Heritage/CAMRA Restoration Award in 1993. Embossed ceilings testify to its Victorian origins, while the cut-glass panel over the bar declaring 'Pale and Burton Ales' reminds us that our ancestors, unfamiliar with today's bland and ubiquitous lagers, had a very different method of classification for the varying styles of beers then available.

The pub's dim lighting is reminiscent of the days when it would have been gas lit, and the small collapsible shelf running the length of the wall opposite the bar conjures up times past when many meals would have been eaten standing up by people in rather more haste than you are likely to be. At the rear is the restaurant area proper. This is the best bit of the pub, divided up into a series of snugs each with the feel of 19th-century railway compartments.

The pub is next to Charterhouse Square, once home to a Carthusian monastery, and from which Charterhouse School takes its name. Suttons Hospital is a survival of the monastery, and the brothers run pre-arranged tours of this alms establishment, which was used by Elizabeth I prior to her coronation. On the opposite side of the square is Florin Court, a fine piece of Art Deco architecture that was used as the exterior of Hercule Poirot's apartments in the television series starring David Suchet as Agatha Christie's Belgian sleuth.

Below: A fry-up and a pint is perhaps not the healthiest breakfast, but the market workers that frequent this superbly restored pub appreciate it.

THE GRAPES

ADDRESS: 76 NARROW STREET, E14
BEERS: BURTON PA, ADNAM'S BITTER, BASS
HOURS: MON–FRI 11AM–11PM; SAT 12 NOON–11PM; SUN 12 NOON–10.30PM

Records show a hostelry on the site of The Grapes in the 16th century, and the present building goes back to a very creditable 1650. One of East London's best known pubs, it is also a noted fish restaurant. The first-floor dining room is known as The Dickens Room in honour of the fact that Charles Dickens is supposed to have used The Grapes as the model for the Six Jolly Fellowship Porters in *Our Mutual Friend*, though there are other riverside pubs – The Prospect of Whitby, for example – that have also claimed this over the years.

A guidebook of 1968 notes that the 'atmosphere is surprisingly cosmopolitan; there are seamen and dockers, tourists and visitors and locals.' Well, the seamen and dockers have gone as the warehouses roundabouts have all been turned into luxury apartments, but The Grapes retains its cosmopolitan atmosphere. This long, narrow pub is divided into two by the staircase to The Dickens Room. A small balcony, sheltered by high-sided wooden screens, allows for stunning views of the ever-changing River Thames, and the equally ever-changing skyline of the Isle of Dogs.

The décor theme is a mixture of Dickensian London and old East End London, plus some river ephemera, all in tastefully subdued tones as is proper for a London pub. Though the inevitable wear and tear has been seen to, The Grapes benefits from not having received too much attention over the years, unlike some of its riverside neighbours.

The Grapes is a great stopping point during an amble along the river, and if you prefer your water rather slower moving than the turbulent Thames then Limehouse Basin, where the Regent's Canal meets the river, is only a short walk away.

Above and opposite: The Grapes is well signed, whichever way you approach it, and is perhaps the most welcoming riverside pub in London.

Below: Whether you just want a quick pint or a blow-out meal at the noted fish restaurant upstairs, a welcoming ambience permeates the whole pub.

THE HAND & SHEARS

ADDRESS: I MIDDLE STREET, ECI
BEERS: COURAGE BEST, COURAGE DIRECTORS, THEAKSTON'S XB
HOURS: MON–FRI IIAM–IIPM

This handsome corner pub was built in 1849, but stands on the site of earlier taverns dating back to the 12th century. Set in the precincts of St Bartholomew's Priory, it was ideally suited to act as the focal point for the cloth fair that took place there and which lent its name to the nearby street. This was held here every year for a fortnight commencing upon St Bartholomew's Day, 24 August. The first cloth fair took place in 1133 and in subsequent years assumed increasing importance, so that traders travelled from all over Europe. As is the way of the City it fell to the guilds to regulate trade in their craft, and by the 16th century it was the job of the Merchant Taylors' Company – first chartered in 1327 – to police the fair. Their official would patrol the fair with a silver standard yard rule to ensure that the City's bylaws and ordinances were upheld. Transgressors were 'tried' at The Hand & Shears, and the usual punishment was a period in the stocks or a flogging. This tradition led to a growing association between the guild and the tavern, so much so that the tavern was allowed to use the Merchant Taylor's badge as its inn sign. Today a stylized version of shears cutting silken cloth is painted over the door.

The last cloth fair was opened by the Lord Mayor of London from the steps of the pub in 1855. Some time before this the principal association of the pub had shifted from cloth cutting to shroud wearing. Newgate Prison was nearby (the site is now the Old Bailey Central Criminal Courts), and when executions were still performed outside its walls The Hand & Shears was the traditional stop for the condemned man to receive his last drop before *the* last drop.

Charles Dickens was a vociferous campaigner against public executions, and after a multiple execution on the roof of the Horsemonger Lane gaol in 1849 he told a friend that he 'felt for some time afterwards almost as if I were living in a city of devils'. In 1868, within Dickens' lifetime, executions in public ceased. Incidentally, it was in 1849, with the construction of the present pub building, that the last-drink custom ceased at The Hand & Shears.

London wags also quip that The Hand & Shears is a reference to the abilities or lack of them of the surgeons of St Bartholomew's Hospital, since these gentlemen are also known to frequent the pub – hence the number of cartoons of a medical theme on the walls.

Left: The imposing inn sign refers to the cloth fair that took place outside the doors of the pub in medieval times – or, as jokers would have it, to the practices of the surgeons at nearby St Bartholomew's Hospital.

THE HARLEQUIN

ADDRESS: 27 ARLINGTON WAY, EC1

BEERS: FULLER'S LONDON PRIDE, TIMOTHY TAYLOR'S LANDLORD

HOURS: MON–SAT 11AM–11PM; SUN 12 NOON–10.30PM

'I have overleaped myself, ladies and gentlemen. I must hasten to bid you farewell; but the pain I feel in doing so is assuaged by seeing before me a disproof of the old adage that familiars have no friends. Ladies and gentlemen, may you and yours ever enjoy the blessings of health is the fervent prayer of Joseph Grimaldi. Farewell!' So saying, the universally regarded father of clowns took his departure from the public arena on 17 March 1828 at Sadler's Wells. Grimaldi first appeared there as an infant dancer in 1781, rising to become stage manager, part owner and one of its biggest attractions. The Harlequin pub, just to the rear of the newly built Sadler's Wells, takes its name from Grimaldi's motley, which he in turn took from the *commedia dell'arte* character, and a transcript of his moving farewell speech takes pride of place in the pub.

Sadler's Wells was built by Thomas Sadler in 1683 as a sideshow for the medicinal well that is still visible on the site. A well recently discovered in The Harlequin's cellar is the most recent of the original wells to have been unearthed. The popularity of the theatre outlived the fashion for taking the waters, however.

The theatre has had a varied history. Between 1844 and 1862, following the breaking of the patent theatre's monopoly over drama, Samuel Phelps produced 34 of Shakespeare's plays there, many of which had not been performed in years. It then had stints as a skating rink, a pickle factory, a boxing rink, and a music hall before closing in 1906.

Lilian Baylis was responsible for resurrecting the fortunes of Sadler's Wells in 1927 and for creating the Royal Ballet; although that company moved to Covent Garden in 1957, Sadler's Wells has been synonymous with dance since Baylis's day.

The simple one-room pub is tastefully decorated with Sadler's Wells memorabilia and there is also a definite Irish theme (look upwards). The landlady, Chrissy, is Irish which explains why her name also appears on the inn sign in the Irish style. The Harlequin is an alehouse of some repute, and the award-winning beer Timothy Taylor's Landlord is always on offer. If one cask runs out another is always ready to go on.

Above and below: Tucked away behind Sadler's Wells Theatre, The Harlequin is visited by dance fans in the know.

HOOP & GRAPES

◆

ADDRESS: 47 ALDGATE HIGH STREET, EC3
BEERS: FULLER'S LONDON PRIDE, ADNAM'S BITTER, WADWORTH 6X, MORLAND'S OLD SPECKLED HEN
HOURS: MON–FRI 11AM–11PM

One of London's most historic inns, the Hoop & Grapes also has one of the best documented histories of any London pub. When it was built in 1598 it took the name The Castle. It is an exceptional building for a number of reasons: it was built of imported softwood, a consequence of the shortage of domestic hardwoods (cooperage was a major drain on hardwood supplies, to the extent that in the mid-16th century Queen Mary had to put a limit on the maximum size of cask that could be used for export).

It survived the Great Conflagration in 1666, and is now the only timber-framed building left in the City, as timber frames were subsequently banned for buildings in order to prevent further devastating fires. Although the building was substantially restored in 1983, the repairers were sensitive to the fact that in 400 years the pub had shifted slightly – some 18 inches in fact, and perhaps it is this 'out of kilter' nature of the building that is its greatest charm.

Aldgate, or 'old gate', was one of London's key thoroughfares and is its most historic. It was one of the six Roman entrances to London, on the road from Colchester. In 1215 the barons came through Aldgate to force King John to sign Magna Carta. Geoffrey Chaucer leased the room over the gate itself between 1374 and 1385. In 1471, during the Wars of the Roses, 5,000 men under the command of the Bastard of Fauconberg were routed when they demanded entry and Londoners lowered the Aldgate portcullis behind them. Mary Tudor entered London here for the first time as Queen; Princess Elizabeth met her with a 2,000-strong guard of honour. The gate was finally demolished in 1761.

Aldgate being just on the borders of the City, traders could supply the City's needs without the fines and fees that accompanied commerce within the City walls. As is usual, various trades gathered in different quarters, and Aldgate became associated with butchers. The area was known as Butchers' Row, it being easier to slaughter animals outside the City walls than in the cramped conditions within. The Hoop & Grapes straddled the borders of the City, being simultaneously in the parish wards of St Botolph Aldgate and St Mary Whitechapel. The ward boundary marker plates are still clearly visible on the party wall to the right of the pub door.

Left: The Hoop & Grapes is a historic treasure chest, having seen armies, monarchs and most of London pass before its ancient timber frame.

THE HOPE

ADDRESS: 94 COWCROSS STREET, EC1
BEERS: YOUNG'S BITTER, YOUNG'S SPECIAL
HOURS: MON–THURS 6AM–9PM; FRI 6AM–11PM

The frontage of The Hope is magnificent and unique, and inside there are glazed tiles of a type once found all over London, and still to be found in several of the pubs in this book. Best of all are the mirrors: though relatively plain in comparison with later Victorian examples (of which, happily, there are plenty of survivors), their simplicity dates them and marks them out as very rare. The back of this recently acquired Young's pub is also rather plain, and is a reminder that for every fine London pub feature that survives countless more have not.

Upstairs on the first floor the sumptuous Sir Loin restaurant (note the 'correct' spelling of sirloin) will lift your heart – gilt chairs, white linen, portraits on the walls – as well as whet your appetite. Thanks to its location next door to Smithfield Market, meat is naturally the main menu item of this traders' pub. Breakfast is served from 7am to cater for the market employees, and the 'Full Celebration Breakfast' includes eggs, bacon, sausages, tomatoes, beans, black pudding, kidneys, liver and, of course, champagne – for two, naturally, for what is the point of drinking champagne alone?

If you are around at this hour of the morning it's well worth venturing into Smithfield Market, one of London's only two remaining wholesale produce markets (the other is Borough Market – see The Market Porter, page 149).

Should you feel a twinge after such a meal – guilt or indigestion – why not slip into the Church of St Bart's the Great just to the south of the market. London's oldest church (1123), it was founded by Rahere,

Right: Many Smithfield deals are done over the unusual breakfast of calves' liver and bacon with champagne for which The Hope is famous.

who also founded St Bart's Hospital. The church's exterior was used in *Four Weddings and a Funeral* and its interior made an appearance in *Shakespeare in Love*. Recently refurbished to the tune of several million pounds, the church looks to have a serious commercial future for many years to come.

When making plans to visit The Hope, remember its unusual opening hours, particularly that it closes early most evenings.

THE JERUSALEM TAVERN

ADDRESS: 55 BRITTON STREET, EC1
BEERS: ST PETER'S BREWERY FULL RANGE
HOURS: MON–FRI 11AM–11PM

The Jerusalem Tavern is one of the most authentic-looking 18th-century tavern-style pubs in London. This is a great tribute to its owners, St Peter's Brewery of Suffolk, and their award-winning architect – for it is, in fact, no such thing. The brewery actually created the tavern from a fine 1720 townhouse that was formerly a coffee shop and then a tea-room, and it is blessed with a great atmosphere.

The windows date from *c.*1840, and the provenance of the dairy-style blue and white tiles on the front walls, which add so much to the feel of the place, was determined only recently. A couple of years ago a lady came into the pub and asked to look at the tiles; her son, she revealed, had made them as part of a commission for a house in the United States. Sadly the sale of the property fell though and the owner's grand plans came to naught and instead they ended up in Clerkenwell. In winter a real fire adds character to the front parlour and it is not unusual to see a party in the parlour periodically rotating, in the style of the Mad Hatter's tea party, in order to allow members of the company to warm up and cool off in turn.

The Jerusalem Tavern is notable for a number of reasons. It may not be authentic but something about it clearly resonates with Londoners. People all across London have heard of it, even if they have not been there and would not know how to find it, and it commands a respect and a following far beyond the local office workers and growing band of Clerkenwell residents who make up its core trade.

For a small pub it can get very busy and will regularly turn over some 30 firkins a week – this is equivalent to seven and a half brewer's barrels or some 2,160 pints, which is going some. The beers all come from the highly individual St Peter's Brewery, which is without doubt the best publicized firm of its size in the British brewing industry. At the tavern you can pick up a brochure on the company, which explains the origins of its distinctive medicine-bottle beers, the highly original recipes used in their extensive beer range, and their top-notch sister operations. You will notice that everything it does is performed with great attention to detail, a fact that Jerusalem regulars are not slow to appreciate.

Below and opposite: This 'modern' pub has recreated a lost 18th-century atmosphere and style very convincingly; it is also renowned for the unique range of microbrewery beers it serves.

LAMB TAVERN

ADDRESS: LEADENHALL MARKET, EC3
BEERS: YOUNG'S BITTER, YOUNG'S SPECIAL, YOUNG'S TRIPLE A
HOURS: MON–FRI 11AM–9.30PM

In some respects the Lamb Tavern is the best manifestation of what the City is about. Sited in the heart of historic Leadenhall Market on Bishopsgate, the City's main thoroughfare, the Lamb offers a glimpse of business as it has been done for centuries: that is, standing up. As you watch the City workers spill out of the doors of the Lamb to drink under the shelter of Sir Horace Jones's 1881 market you are witnessing a pattern of behaviour that has driven the City since Leadenhall Market was first established as a poultry market for 'foreigners' (non-Londoners) in the 14th century. They mill about, flit from group to group, meet old friends, make new introductions, shake hands on a deal, and move on. This is exactly how business was done in Sir Thomas Gresham's Royal Exchange (1567), the Stock Exchange (stock jobbing was first recognized as a trade in 1696) and Lloyd's of London (which originated in Edward Lloyd's coffee house in Tower Street in the 1680s).

The modern Lloyd's building designed by Lord Rogers is directly behind the market, and there is a public lift to an observation platform enabling you to look down inside Lloyd's impressive atrium to see the brokers scurrying about much as they do outside the Lamb. The pub dates back to 1780, though the present structure only goes back to the 1881 development, yet it is still a Grade II star listed building.

Leadenhall Market was sold to the City Corporation in 1411 and was declared a general market for poultry, victuals, grain, eggs, butter and cheese in 1445; wool and leather were added at a later date. The market was destroyed by the Great Fire and then rebuilt around three large courtyards – the first for beef; the second for meal, mutton and lamb (though fishmongers, poulterers and cheesemongers also had stalls); and the third yard was the herb market for fruit and vegetables.

The Morris family have run the Lamb for over 50 years, and will, therefore, remember its use as a film location in the John Wayne movie *Brannigan* (1975), which is but the most notable of its many film and television credits.

Below: City traders working in the nearby Lloyd's building seek tradition and refreshment in the glorious surroundings of the Lamb Tavern in Leadenhall Market.

THE OLD BELL

ADDRESS: 95 FLEET STREET, EC4

BEERS: BRAKSPEAR'S BITTER, FULLER'S LONDON PRIDE, TIMOTHY TAYLOR'S LANDLORD, WADWORTH 6X

HOURS: MON–FRI 11.30AM–11PM

Fleet Street's associations with printing and the press are well known, and it is hard to think of Fleet Street without thinking of the watering holes where generations of hacks have worked hard. None, however, has quite the ink-and-type pedigree of The Old Bell. A former tavern on the site, The Sun, was home to Wynkyn de Worde, former assistant to England's first printer William Caxton (c.1422–91), and de Worde's books were 'emprynted at the sygne of the Sun Flete Strete'.

The present building was designed by Sir Christopher Wren in 1670 as a hostel for workers rebuilding St Bride's Church after the Great Fire of 1666; architectural plans of the church adorn the walls. Unwittingly, Wren anticipated the practice of the 19th-century developers of the London suburbs who would build half a street starting with a pub, in order to claw back the wages of their labourers still engaged in the construction of the rest of the street.

Little is known of the tavern's history in the 18th century, but by 1833 it would seem that the premises were becoming respectable. Richard Etty, the licensee at that time, advertised that he 'continues his old system of cooking viz – Hot Joints daily from 12 to 7 o'clock; also mock turtle and other soups. Superior old wines, spirits, ale, stout etc. of the best quality and lowest terms.' By this time The Old Bell would have been just one among a number of taverns on Fleet Street, since the area was exempt from many of the public ordinances that applied west of Temple Bar (in the Strand) and east of Ludgate; that is, Fleet Street was free to offer all kinds of services not available elsewhere, and not all respectable services either.

By the late 19th century the building was owned by the small Croydon brewery firm of Nalder and Collyer, who resisted the craze of the time for massive investment and refurbishment. This was because they expected The Old Bell to suffer the same fate as many great London inns and be demolished for road widening and sewer building. In the end, only a fraction of the building was lopped off, making it a valuable anthropological survival.

Above and below: The Old Bell is an aristoctrat among London pubs; traditionally a printers' drinking hole, it was designed by no less a figure than Sir Christopher Wren.

OLD RED LION

◆

ADDRESS: 418 ST JOHN STREET, EC1
BEERS: GREENE KING ABBOT ALE, BASS, ADNAM'S BITTER, ADNAM'S BROADSIDE, FULLER'S LONDON PRIDE
HOURS: MON–SAT 12 NOON–11PM; SUN 12 NOON–10.30PM

A 10-minute walk from the King's Head theatre pub in Islington (see page 100) is the Old Red Lion, a bigger pub, but a smaller venue. It is probably fair to say that the Old Red Lion is possibly the more adventurous and experimental of the two. It is also one of the City's liveliest pubs, both in terms of atmosphere and clientele, who are likely to be an arty and independent-minded bunch. This may have something to do with the proximity of City University, some 500 yards away.

The pub proudly proclaims itself to have been on the site since 1415, though the interior is rather more concerned with the here and now than with the styles of the early 15th century or even those of 1899, which is when it was rebuilt. Having said that, you will notice immediately that the pub is split down the middle by a 19th-century partition, and it is obvious that the pub followed the fashion of the day and was subdivided. The lateness of its rebuilding, after the bottom had fallen out of the London pub market, invites speculation, though, as to how the pub would have looked.

The prints on the wall are shots of shows in rehearsal, helpfully arranged in more or less chronological order. By no means all the evening clientele will be theatre visitors – locals, students, office workers, and the occasional soap star can also be found downing pints here – but if you particularly liked an actor's performance there is every chance that you will be able to buy a drink and discuss it with him or her after the show.

Above: The Red Lion incorporates one of London's best-known fringe theatre spaces, and is very popular with local students.

Left: The Old Red Lion is a comfortable pub with few pretensions but plenty of good old-fashioned values.

THE PRIDE OF SPITALFIELDS

ADDRESS: 3 HENEAGE STREET, E1
BEERS: FULLER'S LONDON PRIDE, FULLER'S ESB, REGULAR GUEST ALES
HOURS: MON–SAT 11AM–11PM; SUN 12 NOON–10.30PM

Kerry Butler, then landlord of The Pride of Spitalfields, died on 10 May 1966. On 8 August the staff of the Whitechapel Bell Foundry – the oldest industrial premises in the UK, founded in 1420 – paid him the impressive tribute of ringing a quarter peal of 1260 Plain Bob Minor on the six bells of Nicholas Hawksmoor's Christ Church Spitalfields. A quarter peal of Plain Bob Minor is a considerable amount of bell ringing, and not every publican who dies gets a peal of bells (though there is a strong argument that they should). Kerry Butler, we may deduce, was a much loved and much missed Spitalfields character.

The Pride of Spitalfields is a great little boozer tucked away off the increasingly colourful and trendy Brick Lane. It is an oasis of tranquillity and excellent beer – it serves a wide range of guest ales from Britain's 500-strong army of microbrewers. The pub is a great place to relax and soak up some local history.

It takes its name from the fact that the area was a centre of brick- and tile-making in the 16th century. The Truman Black Eagle Brewery established itself there in the 17th century, and by 1760 the Truman porter brewery was London's third largest brewery company; by 1873 it was the world's largest. Production ceased in 1982 when Truman, Hanbury and Buxton, still run by members of the founding families, became part of Watney's.

Brick Lane is best known as a symbol of successive waves of immigration, and young professionals seem to be the newest immigrants to flood the area. The first were Huguenots fleeing Catholic persecution in France. They settled in Spitalfields and brought silk weaving and textiles to the area. In the 19th century, Jews fleeing European pogroms were the newcomers (hence the 'beigel' shops at the north end of Brick Lane).

The strength of the Jewish community was demonstrated in one of the great events in London's history – the Battle of Cable Street. On Sunday, 5 October 1936 the local populace rioted when Oswald Mosley's British Union of Fascists planned to march through the East End. Mosley was humiliated, but the following week every Jewish shop in the Mile End Road had its windows smashed in London's own *Kristalnacht*. As the Jewish community grew affluent and moved out to north London the Bengalis moved in, and today Brick Lane, south of the brewery, is east London's curry quarter, and The Pride of Spitalfields is right in the middle. Today, the area is the focus of a trendy artistic community, which supports an ever-expanding array of design offices, coffee shops and restaurants.

Right: The Pride of Spitalfields has quite a country-pub feel, and is a quiet oasis just a few steps from bustling cosmopolitan Brick Lane.

PUNCH TAVERN

ADDRESS: 99 FLEET STREET, EC4

BEERS: FULLER'S LONDON PRIDE, ADNAM'S BITTER, GREENE KING ABBOT ALE

HOURS: MON–FRI 11AM–11PM

A few doors away from The Old Bell stands another important Fleet Street pub, the Punch Tavern. Before the days of Rupert Murdoch, when printing presses made up Fleet Street, the Punch was synonymous with printers and newspapers.

Originally called the Crown and Sugarloaf, it became popular with the staff of the once great satirical magazine *Punch*, which was conceived there in 1841. *Punch* folded in the 1990s, to be rescued by the Harrods proprietor Mohammed Al Fayed. His largesse, however, was not endless and the title folded for a second time in May 2002, so proving the truth of the old joke about *Punch* which, supposedly, first started circulating in 1842: '*Punch*. It's not as funny as it used to be.'

When the pub passed into new ownership in the 1890s it was renamed and refurbished in honour of the magazine. By another twist of fate, today's new owners are called

Punch Taverns, one of the country's new superpub companies, and they have refurbished the pub once more. As it was just over a hundred years since the last fit-out, the place probably needed it. On the whole they have done a fairly good and faithful job, with the 1890s feel still much in evidence, along with countless examples of *Punch* humour from the Victorian and Edwardian eras.

It is a great pub interior, starting with the extravagant glazed and tiled lobby, continuing through to the ornate plasterwork, etched glass and huge bevelled mirrors of the saloon and finishing with Art Deco lighting – a mishmash of styles admittedly, but attractive nonetheless.

There is no doubt, however, that the pub has never fully recovered from the departure of the newspapers to the East End and beyond. Indeed, it used to be even larger, being a joint ownership between the two brewing giants, Bass and Sam Smith's of Keighley, Yorkshire. However, a falling out between the two companies only a few years ago resulted in the right-hand (Sam Smith's) side of the pub being abruptly bricked up; the bar actually continues through the wall into a now derelict room. It can only be hoped that the bars will one day be reunited.

Below left*: This superb interior has been faithfully restored to its original Victorian style, and the fine workmanship must be praised.*

Below*: A gilded Mr Punch attracts the eye to the otherwise unassuming entrance on Fleet Street, which gives little away of the opulence beyond.*

THE ROYAL OAK

ADDRESS: 73 COLUMBIA ROAD, E2
BEERS: NO REAL ALES
HOURS: MON–SAT 1PM–11PM; SUN 8AM–10.30PM

If you walk down Columbia Road on a sunny afternoon you will quickly note that it is unlike the surrounding East End. For a start the south side of the street is a constant row of shops, but they are unlikely to be open. The street has a genteel feel and the shops carry arty, crafty names, and you will rapidly discern a theme – vases and pots, which mean flowers. If you are walking down Columbia Road on a sunny afternoon you have, in fact, made a mistake, for the time to go – when everyone goes – is Sunday morning. For Sunday morning is when the famous Columbia Road Flower Market takes place. Right at the heart of the market is The Royal Oak.

The flower market is a successor to Columbia Market, which was the idea of the philanthropist Baroness Burdett-Coutts, who wanted to wean costermongers off the streets. When it opened in 1869 Columbia Market was a quadrangle surrounded by elaborate market buildings, including a galleried mock Gothic hall and a clock tower which chimed a hymn tune every quarter hour. Needless to say, the coster-

Below: Situated in the heart of London's most famous flower market on Columbia Road, The Royal Oak does its best trade on Sunday mornings.

mongers preferred the streets, which is why Columbia Market no longer exists but Columbia Road Flower Market does. The pub opens at 8am on a Sunday to offer breakfast to the market traders and customers, many of whom have been busy buying and selling well before that. As with most London markets, the professionals arrive early and as the morning wears on the public turn up in increasing numbers.

Columbia Road is a place nearly every Londoner has been to at least once. Unlike other London street markets – Portobello Road, for example – which get crowded with casual tourists, the fact that the flower market takes place when most Londoners are still in bed means it is always busy but never overcrowded, and the fact that everyone is there to buy and not just to browse gives it a special buzz. If you do go, linger – as the morning drags on bargains appear.

Not far from Columbia Road is Brick Lane, once home to the Truman Brewery. Not surprisingly, many East End pubs were Truman houses (Charringtons in the Mile End Road was the other big East End brewer, while Whitbread was in the City in Chiswell Street), and equally unsurprisingly breweries tended to develop a house style in their pub refurbishments (they often had their own architectural departments). The Royal Oak is very much a Truman house. Lots of wood panelling, the distinctive Truman type face and the frosted windows all shout Trumans. Visit The Gun in Brushfield Street and count the similar features, or look at The Birdcage at the other end of Columbia Road for another example of a Truman style with its bottle green tiles.

A bit sleepy when the market is not on, vibrant and bustling when it is, The Royal Oak and the flower market are true living London and living links with the London of times past.

THE THREE KINGS

ADDRESS: 7 CLERKENWELL CLOSE, EC1
BEERS: MORLAND'S OLD SPECKLED HEN, FULLER'S LONDON PRIDE, YOUNG'S BITTER
HOURS: MON–FRI 12 NOON–11PM; SAT 7.30PM–11PM

Y ou should not be misled into thinking that in order to be included in this volume pubs have to be historic or picturesque. Eccentric and welcoming will do just as well, and when it comes to these characteristics The Three Kings has them in spades. The pub is fairly traditional on the outside, however, with two windows advertising it as a former Mann, Crossman & Paulin house – a firm that disappeared into the Watney's maw in 1958, proving that this pub has longevity indeed by London standards.

One of the reasons why The Three Kings survived is, perhaps, that for many years Clerkenwell was a not a very fashionable area. Despite being one of the oldest quarters of London – the *Fons Clericorum* or Clerks Wells which gave the area its name date back to the 12th century and were situated where the parish church of St James is now, across the road from the pub – the area was overlooked and neglected. The Karl Marx Memorial Library made its home here in 1933: Lenin had worked in this old Welsh Dissenters School when in exile in 1902.

As is frequently the case with run-down areas, the people who spotted its potential were artists and artisans, a fair share of whom have clearly had a hand in shaping the style and appearance of The Three Kings. A carved rhinoceros head hangs over the mantelpiece, and various ornaments are made out of papier-mâché, including the inn sign, which depicts three kings – King Henry VIII, King Kong and Elvis the King. Each letter of the pub's name represents a different craft or trade to be found in the locality, although engraving does not seem to be represented – despite the fact Clerkenwell is a local centre of engravers, servicing major customers in Hatton Garden's jewellery stores.

The local clientele are a definite change from the suited types to be found in the City pubs further south. Clerkenwell Visitors Centre sits across the street from the pub, next door to the Church of St James, where martyrs of the Reformation are remembered. To the north are the remains of the House of Detention, one of London's early prisons, which is worth a visit though it remains largely unknown to most Londoners; and just a few yards to the south is Clerkenwell Green, dominated by the old Middlesex Sessions House, now a Masonic lodge.

Above and left: *The eclectic and unusual pub signage represents the many artisan groups that practise in Clerkenwell, and this celebration of craftsmanship, both modern and ancient, continues within the pub.*

THE VIADUCT TAVERN

ADDRESS: 126 NEWGATE STREET, EC1
BEERS: ADNAM'S BITTER, FULLER'S LONDON PRIDE, TIMOTHY TAYLOR'S LANDLORD
HOURS: MON–FRI 12 NOON–11PM

Very popular with postal workers from the Giltspur Street depot, The Viaduct is notable for having one of the most striking Victorian pub interiors in the whole of London. The ceiling is ornate lincrusta – a form of lightweight covering made of pressed paper and linseed oil. On the east wall are three remarkable representations of 'Agriculture', 'Banking' and 'Arts'. Sadly, Miss Arts was attacked and shot at by a drunken soldier celebrating the end of the First World War, and she still bears the wound today.

Further back there are some fine mid-Victorian mirrors which are just right for the period of the pub, which was built in 1869 and named after Holborn Viaduct. The viaduct itself, which is also replete with female allegorical figures, was opened by Queen Victoria in the same year as the pub. It is likely that the pub was built in the knowledge that much of the cost would be recouped from the viaduct's construction workers and navvies.

The pub boasts a rare and handsomely carved cashier's office, which is very much a legacy of the early days of the gin palace style and hints at what the pub's original windows may have looked like. A clue to the possible fate of these may be gleaned from the wall of the watch house in Giltspur Street attached to the Church of the Holy Sepulchre, which bears the legend 'built 1791, destroyed 1941, rebuilt 1962'.

The cellars were originally the cells of Newgate Prison which was directly across the road, and the bar staff will happily show them to customers. The pub also boasts not one, but two ghosts: one called Fred, who lives in one of the cells, but has been known to come up to the bar, and the ghost of a prostitute who was murdered here and who enjoys turning off the toilet lights. Famous past patrons include Oscar Wilde who visited during his trial at the Old Bailey, and though you are unlikely to get anything quite as scandalous as his famous case you are well advised, if you have some time, to cross the road to the Old Bailey itself, ring on the bell and ask for admittance to the public gallery, for a Central Criminal Court trial can rank among the best free theatre to be had in London.

Below and opposite: This large pub has a Victorian interior that cannot fail to impress, and the decoration is so ornate that it will hold your attention through several rounds of drinks.

YE OLDE CHESHIRE CHEESE

ADDRESS: WINE OFFICE COURT, 145 FLEET STREET, EC4
BEERS: SAM SMITH'S OLD BREWERY BITTER
HOURS: MON–FRI 11.30AM–11PM; SAT 12 NOON–3PM, 6PM–11PM; SUN 12 NOON–3PM

Ye Olde Cheshire Cheese is a historic London pub that is certainly well worth a visit. This warren of rooms dates from shortly after the Great Fire of London of 1666, when the pub was rebuilt. The site is much older and covers the cellars of the Bishop of Peterborough.

Famous for its associations with Dr Samuel Johnson, the lexicographer, wit and celebrated 18th-century man of letters, the pub remains very much as Johnson would have remembered it. The main bar is splendidly dark, sporting a sawdust floor and a real fire next to which Charles Dickens used to like to sit, beneath the 1829 portrait of a former waiter, William Simpson. To the left of the Gentlemen's Bar is the Chop Room, a traditional-style London 'ordinary' with booths formed by high-backed settles, providing privacy and grandeur simultaneously. On upper floors are other dining rooms, some available for private hire, including the famous Johnson Room. To the rear the Cheese is divided into secluded areas and quiet snugs, with a modern extension behind to cope with the pub's popularity.

The establishment seems to have had several golden eras. In Johnson's day his drinking friends included portraitist Sir Joshua Reynolds, Edward Gibbon of *The Decline and Fall of the Roman Empire* and David Garrick, the actor/manager. A century later came Thomas Carlyle; Alfred, Lord Tennyson; Charles Dickens; John Forster, biographer, historian and journalist; W. M. Thackeray; George Cruikshank, the caricaturist and illustrator; and Wilkie Collins. Later still came Mark Twain, Theodore Roosevelt, Sir Arthur Conan Doyle, G. K. Chesterton, Max Beerbohm and W. B. Yeats. In many ways the true heyday of the pub was the 1920s rather than the 1770s, for it was then regarded as Fleet Street's finest.

For many years the pub owned a foul-mouthed parrot, Polly. On Armistice Day 1918 it imitated the sound of champagne corks popping some 400 times before fainting. When it died in 1926 obituaries were reported in some 200 newspapers around the world, including the *North China Star*.

A great Cheese tradition that has sadly been lost was their Christmas pudding. Of mammoth dimensions, each year it included a portion of the previous year's pudding, making it continuously the world's oldest dish.

Above and left: As its sign purports — and fine but rickety wood-panelled interior confirms — this pub really is 'olde'. The current building dates back to 1667 when the pub was rebuilt after being destroyed in the Great Fire of London.

YE OLDE MITRE TAVERN

ADDRESS: ELY PLACE, EC1
BEERS: BURTON PA, ADNAM'S BITTER, TETLEY
HOURS: MON–FRI 11AM–11PM

By rights this pub should not be in this book – it is such an excellent establishment that people are initiated to the Mitre by swearing never to disclose its location. Being one of the best hidden pubs, however, there is a good chance that even with directions you may never find it and the author will never have to undergo the terrible blood-curdling forfeit that is inflicted on those who break the oath of secrecy. Another, more solid, reason why the Mitre should not be in this book is because, technically, it is part of the demesne of the Bishop of Ely, and until a few years ago its liquor licence was granted by magistrates in Cambridgeshire rather than in London.

The solid chairs in the back bar are from the Bishop's Palace that used to stand nearby. Ely Place became the town residence of the bishops of Ely during the early 14th century, and the first pub was built in 1546 by Bishop Goodrich for palace servants. Indeed, in the front bar is a post carved from a cherry tree (which Queen Elizabeth is reputed to have used as a maypole) that marked the boundary of the bishop's garden and the land 'leased' to Sir Christopher Hatton. In fact, Hatton effectively commandeered the land and paid the bishop the lordly rent of one red rose a year.

The Mitre is full of history, and it is advisable to ask for the printed history which details the full story of the pub, the bishops of Ely and Sir Christopher Hatton, as well as that of the nearby church; the latter, dedicated to St Etheldreda, the 7th-century founder and first abbess of the monastery at Ely, is also well worth a visit.

Nestling behind the famous Hatton Garden jewellery stores, Ye Olde Mitre has been the refuge of many a beau in need of a stiff drink after realizing the extent of the damage inflicted on his wallet by his enamoured. From the upstairs bar it is possible to peer into the windows of jewellers' workshops, where craftsmen create and repair jewellery for Hatton Garden, making this and neighbouring Clerkenwell among the few remaining artisanal quarters in London.

The present pub dates from 1772 and is very much an alehouse in the traditional sense, trading on its excellently kept ales. Space precludes culinary activities any more ambitious than a toasted sandwich, but you will be surprised at how many sandwiches they can turn out. The author is clearly not the only one who can't keep a secret.

Below: The hard-to-find Mitre Tavern is worth seeking out. Once there, enjoy a drink while reading up on the establishment's colourful history.

MARYLEBONE TO BELGRAVIA

This area is the home of the mews pub, born through the aristocracy's desire to keep their staff happy and quiet and the town planners' desire to keep vulgar pubs hidden away. These alehouses have survived the 20th century's changes in society and class structure and now cater for a more wealthy crowd than stablehands and domestic servants – although stablehands from the Hyde Park Riding School still enjoy a drink at its neighbour, The Archery Tavern.

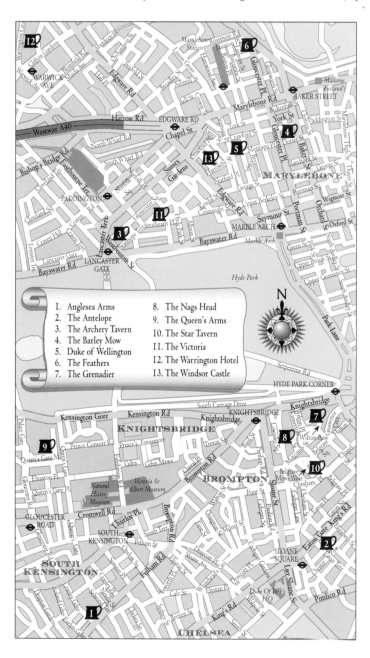

1. Anglesea Arms
2. The Antelope
3. The Archery Tavern
4. The Barley Mow
5. Duke of Wellington
6. The Feathers
7. The Grenadier
8. The Nags Head
9. The Queen's Arms
10. The Star Tavern
11. The Victoria
12. The Warrington Hotel
13. The Windsor Castle

ANGLESEA ARMS

◆

ADDRESS: 15 SELWOOD TERRACE, SW7
BEERS: ADNAM'S BITTER, BRAKSPEAR'S BITTER, BRAKSPEAR'S SPECIAL, FULLER'S LONDON PRIDE, GREENE KING ABBOT ALE
HOURS: MON–SAT 11AM–11PM; SUN 11AM–10.30PM

Built around 1825, the Anglesea Arms lies on the site of a market garden and nursery, which dates back to 1712 and was once owned by a Mr Selwood. In the early 18th century this part of Kensington was a village and several market gardens were in the area, all busy supplying a hungry and ever-expanding London. Appropriately, the road on which the pub sits was named Salad Lane, before becoming Swan Lane and then Selwood Terrace. The road shares literary connections other than William Cobbett, the famous journalist and social commentator, who was a colleague of Mr Selwood. The young Charles Dickens stayed at 11 Selwood Terrace in 1835 and his fiancée Catherine lived round the corner in York Place. Also, D. H. Lawrence lodged at No. 9.

Today, the pub is a genteel, open-plan modern treatment of the Victorian theme. Original features give it its charm, while bare floors and plain wood tables are very much à la mode. To the rear is a dining room, with wood-panelled walls and high-backed chairs, giving it a rather Hanoverian air, and offering a wider menu than that available in the main bar or patio terrace.

Clues to the tastes of the clientele can be gleaned from the presence of a selection of Havana cigars for sale and the wine vintage chart on the pub table cards. Beyond wine, however, the pub has had a reputation for good beers since the 1970s, when it was one of the first free houses to sell real ale from independent brewers.

Major attractions in the area include fine eateries on the Old Brompton Road and excellent shopping on the Fulham Road and King's Road, while further north are the Royal Albert Hall, the Kensington museums and Kensington Gardens.

Left and above left: The Anglesea Arms is a handsome pub with a fine pedigree, and is therefore well suited to its locality — although it started out as a pub serving market gardeners.

Previous pages: Stablehands aplenty would have once visited The Nags Head mews pub (see page 86), while The Archery Tavern (see page 80), still serves stablehands from the nearby Hyde Park Riding School.

THE ANTELOPE

ADDRESS: 22 EATON TERRACE, SW1
BEERS: FULLER'S LONDON PRIDE, ADNAM'S BITTER, GREENE KING IPA, MORLAND'S OLD SPECKLED HEN
HOURS: MON–FRI 11.30AM–11PM; SAT 12 NOON–11PM

The Antelope could only be in SW1. It has a feel about it. You could not pick it up and put it down anywhere else without it looking like a fish out of water. Since it is in just the right place it feels comfortable, and a pub that feels comfortable is a pub that has got it right.

Built as a mews pub, albeit on a corner site, in 1827, when Belgravia was being transformed from an area of notoriety into one of gentility by Thomas Cubitt's major redevelopments, it was intended to cater for a mews clientele: servants, footmen, ostlers and the like, and its essentially spartan character bears witness to this. Its charm is its unaffectedness. It is a place where you come to stand at the bar, gossip and laugh. Those who would like to eat can be catered for at lunchtime, though the old dining room, famously divided into booths, is no longer in operation.

The Antelope is very much a locals' pub, after its own fashion, and whereas pubs in east or south London might have a prize draw, or a meat raffle, or a pool league to act as a point of common interest, The Antelope has a cricket club: the walls are decorated with team photos and the club roll of honour.

The pub itself is fairly small, with a large island bar. A small, snug-like room to the left compensates for any overcrowding at busy times, and to the rear are old-fashioned settle-type seats of the kind that were once the hallmark of the alehouse, but which are all too rare today. The Antelope is wonderfully unspoilt.

Below: The large island bar defines The Antelope and makes conversation with your neighbours, whether you know them or not, very much the done thing — hence the convivial atmosphere.

THE ARCHERY TAVERN

ADDRESS: 4 BATHURST STREET, W2
BEERS: BADGER BITTER, TANGLEFOOT, KING AND BARNES SUSSEX
HOURS: MON–SAT 11AM–11PM; SUN 12 NOON–10.30PM

The site upon which The Archery Tavern now stands was once part of the estate of the bishop of London. In 1818 one Thomas Waring leased four acres of this land at £7 per acre for use as archery butts, at a time when archery was enjoying a vogue as a leisure pastime for the well-to-do. Archery is more properly known as toxophily, and the Toxophilite Society moved to Waring's butts in 1821 after their original home in the gardens of Leicester House (now Leicester Square) was demolished. Waring's lease expired in 1828, but a map of 1832 shows a slightly smaller plot of land still in use over an area now bordered by Bayswater Road and Westbourne Street, Sussex Square and part of Sussex Terrace.

The Royal Toxophilite Society, which still exists today, was founded in 1781 by the employer of Thomas Waring's father. Waring Senior had taken up archery around 1774 as a remedy for a chest complaint; his employer followed his example and so enjoyed the sport that he decided to formalize it. The Warings spent many years promoting the sport, and Waring Junior even exported his archery equipment to America from 1829.

The toxophilists left Waring's butts in 1834, and bowling became the fashionable activity until 1839 when development put paid to all forms of outdoor recreation on the site. The landlord, James Bott, then built himself The Archery Tavern between 1839 and 1840. The decision to maintain the archery connection was Bott's and has been upheld to this day: the inn sign depicts Thomas Waring Jnr.

The Archery Tavern itself is a happy find in a part of town not brimming with pubs. It is suitably handsome and genteel, with the archery theme subtly, but not overly, present throughout. It is clearly a pub with a good local following, and Bathurst Street is sufficiently tucked away behind the Bayswater Road to leave the main body of tourists behind. From the pub you would join the Bayswater Road at the Marlborough Gate and West Carriage Drive, where Hyde Park becomes Kensington Gardens; this is also the point at which the underground River Westbourne briefly surfaces to become the Serpentine.

Below: You are more likely to find stablehands than archers drinking in the 1840 Archery Tavern these days, thanks to the working stables of the Hyde Park Riding School in the mews next door.

THE BARLEY MOW

ADDRESS: 8 DORSET STREET, W1
BEERS: GREENE KING IPA, MARSTON'S PEDIGREE, TETLEY
HOURS: MON–SAT 11AM–11PM

The Barley Mow sits on Dorset Street, which takes its name from the home county of the Portman family who owned the local estate. The next street, Blandford, takes its name from the Dorset town of Blandford St Mary, today the home of the Hall and Woodhouse Brewery, several of whose pubs, selling their Badger beer, feature in this book. Three streets further south is Portman Square, which was, until 2001, home to the Brewers Society (latterly known as the British Beer and Pubs Association) and eponymous home to the Portman Group, the brewing industry watchdog.

With all these local brewing connections, therefore, it is entirely appropriate that The Barley Mow should have a fine history and pedigree. The pub itself was built in 1791 and is named for the fields that were once situated around the small agricultural community of Marylebone. Although it is hard to believe now, this was once a farmers' pub. The inn sign celebrates the tradition of drinking over a sheaf of barley when the harvest was fully gathered in.

The pub is a few minutes' walk from Regent's Park, the remnants of an old hunting ground that was remodelled and laid out as parkland by the architect John Nash. The pub's early customers consisted of the grooms and footmen to the wealthy occupants of Nash's Regency terraces that edge the park.

In those days it was common, indeed inevitable, that landlords extended a certain amount of credit, and many acted as unofficial pawnbrokers. Pawnbroker shops were traditionally divided into booths in order to ensure privacy for the poor souls driven to pledge their possessions to raise a few shillings (often to be spent on gin), and pawnbroker booths are now a unique

feature of The Barley Mow. Ironically the pawnbroker's booth was also the inspiration for the development of the snug and the ornately partitioned pubs of the 1870s such as The Argyll Arms (see page 18). These embellishments were sadly short-lived in many pubs as magistrates began to demand greater openness in public houses, but luckily those in The Barley Mow survived.

Right: The Barley Mow, which dates back to the late 18th century, claims to be the oldest pub in Marylebone. Its huge sign tells something of its agricultural past.

DUKE OF WELLINGTON

◆

ADDRESS: 94A CRAWFORD STREET, W1
BEERS: FULLER'S LONDON PRIDE, ADNAM'S BITTER
HOURS: MON–SAT 11AM–11PM; SUN 12 NOON–10.30PM

Just round the bend in the road from The Windsor Castle (see page 91), where Crawford Place becomes Crawford Street, is another must-visit pub. Once you know that the landlord of the one is also the landlord of the other, things will start to fall into place.

The Duke of Wellington is a bizarre pub that also doubles as a museum. This comfortable one-roomed house is a shrine to the hero of Waterloo. Every possible surface contains memorabilia of some form or another, from tiny lead soldiers to a full-size Roman-style bust of the great general and politician. Most of this is arranged in display cases in the windows and, as at The Windsor Castle, this memorabilia alone makes the two pubs among the most fascinating in London. Wellington's great adversary Napoleon gets a look in, too. Others of the Duke's campaigns are covered, in particular the Peninsular Campaign, during which his distinguished conduct elevated him from humble Lord Wellesley to the exalted national hero.

If you spend any time in the Duke of Wellington you are likely to have your curiosity aroused by this enigmatic character. The best place to fill the gaps in your knowledge is at the end of the Edgware Road and across Hyde Park, for at Hyde Park Corner you will find Apsley House, once the Duke's residence. He used to refer to this as No. 1 London, though what the King thought of this little conceit is not known. It is said that the Duke was forced to leave the shutters on the ground-floor windows closed, as whenever they were opened a crowd would gather to peer in at Boney's nemesis.

Above and below: The Duke is an Aladdin's cave of curios and knick-knacks, all themed around the Iron Duke and his arch-enemy, Boney.

THE FEATHERS

ADDRESS: 43 LINHOPE STREET, NW1
BEERS: FLOWERS ORIGINAL, FULLER'S LONDON PRIDE
HOURS: MON–SAT 12 NOON–11PM; SUN 12 NOON–10.30PM

One of the charms of a city of eccentricities such as London is that even experienced Londoners do not know everything and can still be surprised by serendipitous discovery. Very few, therefore, beyond those who live or work in the immediate environs of Linhope Street, will know about The Feathers. This is just as well because The Feathers must be the smallest pub in London. If 20 people walked in all at once, one would be left standing and the rest would be rather cosy.

This little backstreet boozer, in a residential area just off Dorset Square and only 200 yards away from Marylebone Station, is full of charm. This charm is derived, in part, from the fact that the thousands of commuters that daily use London's quietest and friendliest mainline terminus are oblivious to its existence. This little quarter of London did achieve 15 minutes of fame in 1975, however, when IRA terrorists held a couple hostage at 22B Balcombe Street, just behind The Feathers. The six-day police seige dominated the news until the terrorists surrendered, leaving their hostages unharmed.

The Feathers is well worth seeking out if you are looking for refreshment in this part of the world, in particular because most of the pubs east of Linhope Street are nowhere near as good. The Clarence Gate of Regent's Park is a two-minute walk away, and a drink in The Feathers would be an ideal aperitif for a performance in the famous open-air theatre. If you are planning to see *A Midsummer Night's Dream* you would best go well fortified with a warming malt whisky for when the sun goes down.

Right: This tiny pub in a delightful part of London all too often gets passed by, making it a good choice for those seeking to escape London's madding crowd.

THE GRENADIER

ADDRESS: OLD BARRACK YARD, WILTON ROW, SW1
BEERS: COURAGE BEST, COURAGE DIRECTORS, MARSTON'S PEDIGREE, MORLAND'S OLD SPECKLED HEN
HOURS: MON–SAT 12 NOON–11.30PM; SUN 12 NOON–10.30PM

The Grenadier is one of that select band of pubs that people deliberately seek out as destinations in their own right. In this case the particular attraction is the Bloody Mary for which the pub is internationally famous. On a Sunday lunchtime there is even a special Bloody Mary bar, behind which a usually overworked barman turns out a constant supply of the spicy cocktails as fast as he can shake them. On their best ever Sunday they managed to serve some 300 – that's some shaking.

Tucked away behind Wilton Crescent off Belgrave Square, the pub was originally the Duke of Wellington's officers mess, and outside in Old Barrack Yard are the remains of the duke's mounting block and stables. The pub was then known as The Guardsman and was popular with King George IV. In later years it became The Grenadier and is still popular with officers of that regiment when they are on ceremonial duties at the nearby royal palaces.

The pub itself is quite small and adorned with guards mementoes and memorabilia. The pewter bar is original, extremely rare and may be the oldest of its kind. A narrow ledge runs around the bar area for people to rest their drinks on, as there is very little by way of seating. To the rear is a restaurant which specializes in traditional English fare. Naturally, Beef Wellington is a favourite. On sunny days most customers will spill out into Wilton Row to enjoy their drinks, which are frequently accompanied by another speciality of the pub, a sausage on a stick served with a dollop of ketchup and a dollop of mustard.

Britain boasts many haunted pubs, but London remarkably few, maybe because your average ghost is no match for your average Cockney. The Grenadier is an exception, and is reported to be haunted each September by a guards officer who died when overenthusiastically flogged for cheating at cards. The Grenadier is an ideal spot to perk yourself up after a visit to the Duke of Wellington's residence, Apsley House at Hyde Park Corner.

Below and right: The Grenadier is famous for Bloody Marys and at least one bloody death, hence its reputation for being haunted by the ghost of a card-cheat officer.

THE NAGS HEAD

ADDRESS: 53 KINNERTON STREET, SW1
BEERS: ADNAM'S BITTER, ADNAM'S REGATTA, ADNAM'S BROADSIDE
HOURS: MON–SAT 11AM–11PM; SUN 12 NOON–10.30PM

'The upstairs bar was designed about a hundred years ago to encompass the frame of one working man at a time. Today this same bar is forced to accommodate 40 or 50 gentlemen, often with the effect that one of them may be expelled into the street with the velocity of an orange pip angrily fired from between the thumb and forefinger of an ill-disposed gorilla.' So wrote one rather excitable fan of this truly great pub in 1963, when it could still uphold its claim to being the smallest pub in London. If an ill-disposed gorilla did choose to frequent The Nags Head it is unlikely that it would raise much comment. The locals are an eccentric enough bunch themselves and tend to take folk pretty much as they find them.

Built in 1775, Kinnerton Street was a row of stables, and the tavern may have been added in the 1820s. The walls of The Nags Head are a mass of in-jokes, caricatures and cartoons of regulars, including former local, the actor James Mason. There is a small, fine collection of antique amusement machines of Allwins and the end-of-the-pier variety, while a shelf at picture-rail level is crammed with pub clutter of the finest quality.

The pub is most unusual in that the bar service area is lower than the floor, meaning that the staff are looking up at you, and the bar counter itself must be one of the lowest in Britain. Pride of place on the bar belongs to a fine antique beer engine, which still sees service dispensing three Adnam's ales.

At the rear is a larger room, down a short flight of stairs, but the locals tend to prefer the top bar, and it is the locals who really make this pub, and will happily drag you into a conversation.

With real fires adding to the cheery glow, The Nags Head is a delightful place to while away an hour or two, all to soundtracks from the 1930s and 1940s. The best time to visit is on a lazy Sunday when the locals pretty much have the place to themselves and Kinnerton Street seems to forget that it's in central London.

Below: The Nags Head is famous for having the lowest bar top in London; this highly unusual feature is due to the sunken serving area behind and is accommodated for with tiny bar stools.

THE QUEEN'S ARMS

ADDRESS: 30 QUEEN'S GATE MEWS, SW1
BEERS: FULLER'S LONDON PRIDE, BASS
HOURS: MON–SAT 11AM–11PM; SUN 12 NOON–10.30PM

Considering how much there is to do and see in South Kensington it is remarkable how few pubs there are in the neighbourhood, and of those how few are even half decent. The best, by far, is The Queen's Arms, tucked away in Queen's Gate Mews. Perhaps it is this out-of-the-way location that has saved it, but certainly you need to know it is there as a chance encounter is unlikely.

This mews pubs was intended, as readers who have encountered other mews taverns will by now know, to serve the countless servants of the wealthy families who lived in 19th-century Kensington. Little by way of original features remain in this large one-bar boozer located opposite an exclusive dealership of vintage cars. In summer it is possible to spill out of the pub and enjoy your drink while gazing enviously at an array of bright shiny Lagondas, Bugattis and Aston Martins: a reminder that some things are just not meant to be enjoyed by everyone.

What *was* built to be enjoyed by everyone was the Royal Albert Hall, some three minutes' walk away. Queen Victoria laid the foundation stone on the site of the former Grove House on 20 November 1868 and she returned to declare the building open on 29 March 1871. In the years since, countless millions have followed in her footsteps in order to see the big-name acts of the day.

The Queen's Arms is *the* place to go after a concert, but do not dawdle on leaving the hall as the pub fills up extremely fast making it difficult to get served.

Above and below: Like many of London's best pubs, The Queen's Arms is tucked away. Although it rarely receives passing trade, true pub lovers will make a point of seeking it out.

THE STAR TAVERN

ADDRESS: 6 BELGRAVE MEWS WEST, SW1

BEERS: FULLER'S CHISWICK BITTER, FULLER'S LONDON PRIDE, FULLER'S ESB, FULLER'S SEASONAL ALE

HOURS: MON–FRI 11AM–11PM; SAT 12 NOON–3PM, 6.30PM–11PM; SUN 12 NOON–3PM, 7PM–10.30PM

It is easy to imagine liveried footmen and jodhpured stable lads taking their ease before the real fire in The Star Tavern, as it has something of the tack room about it. It is almost certain that such characters would have been the principal customers when this handsome Georgian mews pub was built.

One can be in little doubt that this is a Fuller's house since mirrors, signs and plaques shout the brand at you everywhere you look. The right side of the pub consists of the bar, where the regulars congregate, and the other side opens out to a long, broad, airy room divided in two by a gentle arch. Both sides are warmed by a rare solid-fuel fireplace. On the first floor is a dining room which has the distinct feel of a gentleman's library.

The pub does remarkably good business even at weekends, given that it is not in a hugely residential area, being located to the rear of Belgrave Square, the heart of London's diplomatic quarter. Indeed, it is very much a destination pub, and is doubtless commonly recommended by the doormen and concierges of the Knightsbridge hotels, judging by the number of foreign visitors who manage to find it. Actually, there is no shortage of first-rate recommendations in this neighbourhood, for also tucked behind Belgrave Square one can find The Nags Head (see page 86) and The Grenadier (see pages 84–85).

Belgrave Square takes its name from a Leicester village and was laid out in 1826 when the Earl of Grosvenor obtained an Act of Parliament allowing him to build there. Developed by Thomas Cubitt, it was the design of a pupil of the great London architect Sir John Soane, George Basevi, cousin to the future prime minister Benjamin Disraeli. Damp clay was dug from the ground and made into bricks on the site, and the workings were filled in with soil from the excavation of St Katharine's Dock (see Dickens Inn, page 54).

Nearby attractions include Buckingham Palace, Hyde Park, Apsley House, Harrods and Harvey Nichols, all of which are only five minutes' walk from The Star.

Below: The Star Tavern has a strong local following but also attracts visitors from far and wide. It is one of Fuller's Brewery's top houses.

THE VICTORIA

ADDRESS: 10A STRATHEARN PLACE, W2
BEERS: FULLER'S CHISWICK BITTER, FULLER'S LONDON PRIDE, FULLER'S ESB
HOURS: MON–SAT 11AM–11PM; SUN 12 NOON–10.30PM

If you emerge from either Lancaster Gate or Marble Arch tube stations and enter the triangle of land bordered by the Bayswater Road, Sussex Gardens and the Edgware Road, you will find yourself in Tyburnia, so named to rival Fitzrovia at the other end of Oxford Street. It takes its name from the Tyburn gallows which were originally sited near Bond Street tube, where Stratford Place meets Oxford Street. As the city expanded the gallows gradually moved west and ended up at Tyburn Tree, where Edgware Road meets Marble Arch. Speakers' Corner in Hyde Park owes its origins as a place of free speech to the proximity of Tyburn, for the simple reason that if you were about to execute someone in public there were precious few sanctions left at your disposal to prevent them from saying what happened to be on their mind.

Above: A stunning example of high-Victorian style, The Victoria is not without its own royal pretensions, and the long-lived 19th-century monarch and her family are celebrated all over the walls.

Just round the corner from Westbourne Street is The Victoria, a pub with a truly magnificent interior. This luxurious Victorian tavern, with its sumptuously ornate mirrors and a carved bar back, achieved some fame in the 1960s when a painting on the wall was discovered to be a valuable portrait of a member of the royal family; it is now part of the Royal Portrait Collection. Today, royal portraits are not in short supply at the Victoria – Queen Victoria, her consort and her children appear over the fireplace at the west end of the pub, balancing the large mirror at the other end of the room. The size of the room and the contrasting style of its two fireplaces suggest that it may once have been split into two.

There are many items of interest to be found at this establishment, and it repays careful examination. In the bar there are superb mirrors that continue the royal theme with their fleur-de-lys pattern, and hunt out the unusual tiles that can be found above the wall-hung prints. Don't miss the upstairs 'Library', which is a delightful place for a private function, and the 'Theatre Bar', complete with lots of theatrical memorabilia and having very much the feel of a West End theatre bar.

Right: The Victoria acts as a bookend to a terrace of grand cream-painted houses, and is prettily adorned with hanging baskets and well-kept plants.

THE WARRINGTON HOTEL

ADDRESS: 93 WARRINGTON CRESCENT, W9
BEERS: FULLER'S LONDON PRIDE, GREENE KING IPA, YOUNG'S BITTER, GUEST ALES
HOURS: MON–SAT 11AM–11PM; SUN 12 NOON–10.30PM

An impressive frontage greets those turning into the broad sweep of Warrington Crescent: pillars of Babylonian intricacy form the main approach to the pub. Step over the Romanesque mosaic bearing the pub's name and enter a rich and unique interior. Not all is authentic in this Edwardian hostelry, but the later additions are either sufficiently well executed or sufficiently tongue in cheek to get away with it. Note in particular the Aubrey Beardsley-esque mock Art Nouveau nudes that adorn the carved awning over the beautifully complex bar: in a faux-marquetry style, they turn out to have been painted by Colin Beswick in 1965 and work exceptionally well.

Satisfyingly dark woods interact with dark reds in the carpets and William Morris-style wallpaper on the ceiling to give the correct patina to the pub. The darkness is broken up by mirrors, which in turn are divided by carved wooden mouldings, and doors and screens with stained glass that combines Art Nouveau with more classical designs.

Facing the bar, marble pillars support intricately carved wooden arches, which guide the eye to the heavily balustraded staircase leading up to the Thai restaurant on the first floor, one of the first of several Thai restaurants to have made a home in London pubs.

Built in 1859 and remodelled in the 1990s, the pub was originally a hotel, albeit one with a dubious reputation — it was allegedly a brothel, which must have caused some consternation to its owners, the Church of England. The pub was also a famous haunt of jockeys and members of the racing fraternity, one of whom once won £100 by riding a horse up the steps and into the pub.

Above and below: Over the years the behaviour of patrons of The Warrington has been dilletantish, dashing and debauched, but with an interior like this, what else could have been expected?

THE WINDSOR CASTLE

ADDRESS: 27–29 CRAWFORD PLACE, W1
BEERS: ADNAM'S BITTER
HOURS: MON–SAT 11AM–11PM; SUN 12 NOON–10.30PM

The Windsor Castle is one of the great hidden pubs of London. Although it is just off the busy Edgware Road it is unknown to all but a few who pass that way. This is a pub just as people would like to imagine pubs to be, beautifully eccentric and a total confection of all the landlord's whims and fancies. If the locals like it too, then all the better. In this case the landlord's fancies clearly include the British royal family. Seemingly every commemorative mug and plate produced for a royal event over the last 70 years is on display here. Entire walls are devoted to royal family prints.

Above head height are a number of signed prints of film stars and celebrities who have been as charmed by The Windsor Castle as you will be. The windows are stuffed with eclectic collections: coloured sands, porcelain bottle stoppers and glass ashtrays with a royal theme; Toby jugs crowd the shelves; there are vintage bottled beers, cameos, and even the tables double up as a history lesson. And all of these delights are accompanied by 1940s soundtracks.

Not surprisingly, this is a pub that attracts devotees. The names of many of them, past and present, are engraved on brass plates screwed to the bar. The Handlebar Club meets there on the first Friday of the month. This is, of course, the club for gentlemen sporting stupendous handlebar moustaches, some of which are several feet in length.

This is a superbly English pub – once inside you are spirited away to a land of deference and good manners. However, incongruously with the rest of its character, the pub does serve good Thai food, either in the bar or upstairs.

The Windsor Castle is the kind of pub that just grows better the more you learn about it, and it certainly bears repeat visits. When the locals are in you might even start to believe that there is good in the world, and all cynicism starts to dissipate. If you visit only five pubs in London make sure that The Windsor Castle is one of them.

Below: National pride exudes from The Windsor Castle, and although some may find the hectic interior overwhelming, it is undeniably engrossing.

North London

It being in the nature of Man to divide into nations, nations to divide into tribes and tribes into clans, it is not surprising that within a fiercely proud city such as London there is a strong rivalry between south and north Londoners. Northerners deride the south for its lack of tube lines and permanently congested South Circular ring-road, while southerners point to north London's absence of decent pubs. Although much of north London is a publess urban sprawl, there are still plenty of pubs in its leafy villages, such as Highgate and Hampstead, and some of these are among the best the metropolis has to offer. Whether you choose to visit the pseudo-coaching inn that is The Albion in Islington or head slightly further afield to Hampstead's famous and infamous Spaniards Inn, you won't be disappointed.

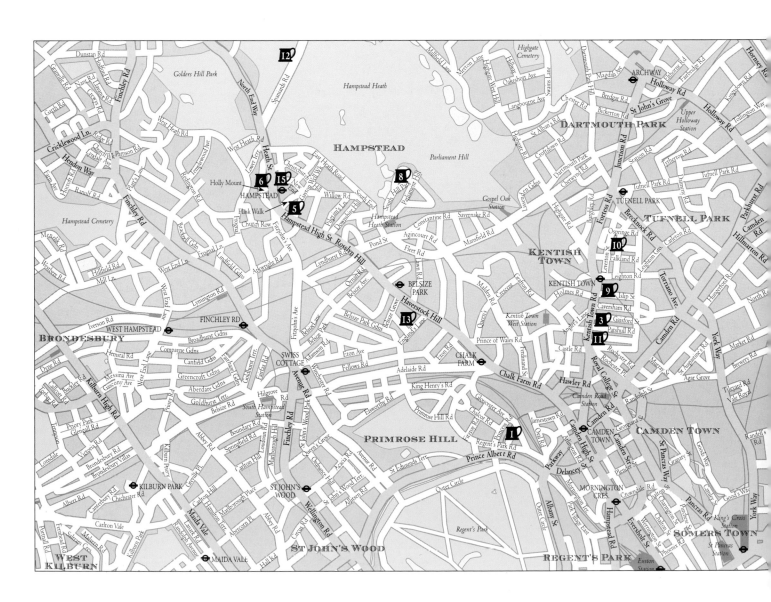

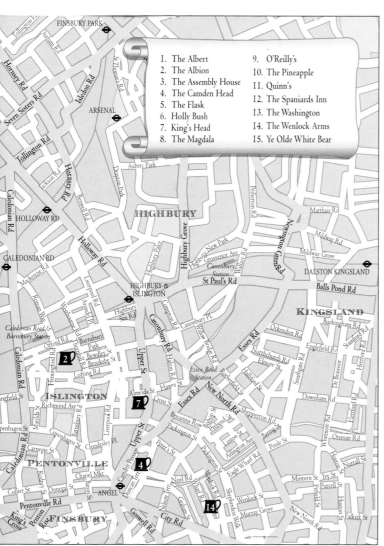

1. The Albert
2. The Albion
3. The Assembly House
4. The Camden Head
5. The Flask
6. Holly Bush
7. King's Head
8. The Magdala
9. O'Reilly's
10. The Pineapple
11. Quinn's
12. The Spaniards Inn
13. The Washington
14. The Wenlock Arms
15. Ye Olde White Bear

THE ALBERT

ADDRESS: 11 PRINCESS ROAD, NW1
BEERS: FULLER'S LONDON PRIDE, BASS, GREENE KING IPA
HOURS: MON–SAT 11AM–11PM; SUN 12 NOON–10.30PM

The Albert is a medium-size Victorian pub which has received the modern treatment in a most sympathetic and successful fashion. Bare wood floors and a motley crew of non-matching wooden tables and chairs in different styles are very much in the modern style, as are the fresh flowers on each table. The history is confined to the walls and ceiling, and very handsome they are too. To the rear is an airy conservatory, leading out to a sizeable and very secluded garden which takes a spreading apple tree as its focal point.

Food is very much the business of the pub, which specializes in modern British cooking at pub prices. Built in the 1860s, the pub was named after the then recently deceased consort of Queen Victoria. Albert was a hugely popular figure, and his considerable energies and dynamism as a modernizer and proactive champion of innovation were both recognized and appreciated. A glimpse of this may be seen on the walls, where a number of informatively annotated Albert-related prints demonstrate the measure of the man.

The Albert's lovely garden is a great place to soak up the sun, but if you decide you want some more space then Regent's Park is nearby. The pub is also suitably located for enjoying many other north London attractions: the bargain-shopping delights of Camden Market; Primrose Hill is a local beauty spot; and London Zoo – a good full-day attraction which should leave you with an appetite that the Albert can do justice to.

Previous page: The Albion (top) is very much a country pub in town, and The Pineapple (bottom) is popular with the local rich and famous.

Above and below: The Albert is a great place to get modern British food in a traditional English atmosphere.

THE ALBION

ADDRESS: 10 THORNHILL ROAD, N1
BEERS: FULLER'S LONDON PRIDE
HOURS: MON–SAT 11AM–11PM; SUN 12 NOON–10.30PM

There are still cobblestones in the little village-like corner of Islington in which the Albion lives. It is a handsome Regency-style inn, although little of this is visible beneath the thatch of vegetation – ivy, wisteria, hanging baskets and window boxes – that covers the whole. Unsurprisingly, the pub has won quite a few London in Bloom awards.

This large pub has very much the feel of a county hotel in a market town. This is not just because of the portico but because of the size and the layout, too. There are flagstones on the floor, secluded corners with armchairs which give the impression that afternoon tea is about to be served, and dark nooks near the kitchen where in days gone by a poacher might have sidled in to surreptitiously slip the chef a pheasant or a rabbit in exchange for a drink.

To the rear is a sizable garden, shaded by a large wisteria supported by a pergola. The style of the building suggests it was a coaching inn, as is depicted on the inn sign, though you should take care to spot the sign's deliberate mistake. It is, however, doubtful that it ever was a coaching inn, due to the fact that it has never been on a coaching route – although the main route to Liverpool did pass quite close by.

The Albion is a popular locals' pub, and well known in the Islington and Barnsbury area as a handy alternative to the constantly busy pubs of Upper Street.

Above and below: The creeper-clad Albion is in the style of an old country pub; the sizeable bar makes getting a round in all the easier.

THE ASSEMBLY HOUSE

ADDRESS: 292–4 KENTISH TOWN ROAD, NW5
BEERS: MORLAND'S OLD SPECKLED HEN, GREENE KING IPA, RUDDLES COUNTY
HOURS: MON–SAT 12 NOON–11PM; SUN 12 NOON–10.30PM

The Assembly House takes its name from a building of 1796 that was a meeting point for people gathering together to make up a party before setting off for Hampstead Heath and other places north – the occasionally vain hope was that travelling in numbers would deter the highwaymen who infested the woods and lanes along the roads at this time (see The Spaniards Inn, page 106).

This beautiful old late Victorian pub, has, like thousands of others, reinvented itself to perform under modern conditions and appeal to the modern eye. As is often the case, the ceiling provides the best clues as to how this massive space was formerly arranged. A little inside knowledge always helps, too. The area under the glass dome – note the mid-Victorian glass at odds with that elsewhere – was originally a billiard room; on the other side of the chimneypiece was the dining room; what is now the narrowest part of the bar was once a private members' room; and the area that is now set lower than the rest was a public bar. All in all, it forms a very fine example of late Victorian pub architecture.

A particularly striking feature of The Assembly House is its considerable size. Such Victorian pubs needed large spaces to accommodate the large number of activities that went on in them as well as the large number of staff employed.

Original features have been retained, yet the pastel walls, easy chairs, settees and a lighter use of contemporary materials, prints and colours in the front bar give the place that feeling of ease that both translates the pub's historic function into the modern day and makes for a friendly space. This latter consideration has had a huge influence on the appearance of pubs (country inns excluded): now that women constitute over 50 per cent of the workforce and their disposable income has increased dramatically over the last 30 years it is a commercial necessity to appeal to them. Pubs you cannot see into from outside are a dwindling proportion of the total pub stock, yet within living memory they were all like that. The Assembly House is a good example of how the feel of even a grand old Victorian gin palace can be softened up.

Above and left: Londoners tend to forget that their public houses often provide some of the finest architectural features in the city; it is often worth standing back from the building to absorb it as a whole. Inside The Assembly House original features have been treated sympathetically alongside modern refurbishment.

THE CAMDEN HEAD

◆

ADDRESS: CAMDEN PASSAGE, N1
BEERS: COURAGE BEST, COURAGE DIRECTORS, CHARLES WELLS BOMBARDIER
HOURS: MON–SAT 11AM–11PM; SUN 12 NOON–10.30PM

Upper Street, the start of the Great North Road, is a long, straight mile of little else but restaurants and pubs. The restaurants are pretty good – New Labour was hatched in one of them, Granita, when Tony Blair and Gordon Brown were merely Young Bloods with an idea. Just off Upper Street, however, it is a different story, Camden Passage is a little enclave of antique and curiosity shops.

The Camden Head is a magnificently preserved Victorian gin palace with more than its fair share of interesting features. There is a rare pair of water taps on the bar enabling customers to add just the right-size drop of the only thing you are allowed to add to malt whisky apart from more malt whisky. There is a pair of gin globes, sadly incomplete, but exceptionally rare none the less, and there are fine tiles, mirrors and an impressive back bar, or stillion.

There is also a theme: casual perusal will reveal a connection with music hall. A few yards away on Islington Green, in what is now a branch of Waterstone's bookshop, once stood the Collins Music Hall, which functioned from 1862 to 1958, making it London's last operating music hall. The building was gutted in 1963. The connection between this music hall and The Camden Head was clearly symbiotic. Indeed, as The Camden Head is home to one of London's many pub comedy clubs, which are merely music hall in modern garb and which seem to have multiplied consistently in the last decade, the wheel might be said to have come full circle.

The Camden Head allows one to enjoy the best of what Islington has to offer without having to contend with the scrum of Upper Street. The Screen on the Green, one of London's most intimate cinemas, is nearby; the Regent's Canal is reached by ambling down Duncan Street; the Business Design Centre is one of the powerhouses that contribute to Islington's trendy dynamism, in sharp contrast to the traditional outdoor London life of nearby Chapel Market. For those seeking theatrical pleasures, the King's Head Theatre (see page 100) is only a stone's throw away, and Sadler's Wells is just two stones' throws.

Below: At The Camden Head the public house meets the music hall in harmonious symphony; the pub is a wonderfully authentic period gem.

THE FLASK

ADDRESS: 14 FLASK WALK, NW3
BEERS: YOUNG'S BITTER, YOUNG'S SPECIAL, YOUNG'S TRIPLE A
HOURS: MON–SAT 11AM–11PM; SUN 12 NOON–10.30PM

The Flask owes its name to a philanthropic bequest of 1689 when 'six acres of waste land lying and being about certain medicinal waters called the wells' were given over to the benefit of the poor of Hampstead. The wells being the only positive feature of the land, the trustees of the bequest hit on the idea in 1700 of bottling the water and selling it to the public at three pence a flask. The margins on bottled water in the 18th century being every bit as huge as they are in the 21st, the waters were carted to the Thatched House, as the pub was then called, bottled and despatched throughout London to quench the thirst and ease the pains of the upper classes. This was the century of the spa towns such as Bath and Tunbridge Wells – so not surprisingly Hampstead became fashionable, and has remained so ever since.

Remarkably, The Flask remained thatched until 1874, when the building was replaced. Today, the pub is divided into four distinct areas. The front saloon contains the original features, including five painted panels dating from the 1880s, which are unusual in that they follow no particular theme. To the rear is a rather more contemporary drinking area, opening up to a conservatory added in 1990 and decorated with a range of French prints (see if you can spot the one that is also in The Spread Eagle, (page 135). At the front is a simpler public bar, separated from the saloon by the same screen that supports the painted panels. In the public bar these panels are filled with tasteful prints of old Hampstead.

Lino floors and no frills mark out The Flask as one of the dwindling number of pubs that maintain a definite difference between the public and saloon bars. At one time this would have been underlined by the fact that beer bought in the public bar would have been a penny or two cheaper.

The pleasures of Hampstead Heath are only a short walk away, and there are further pubs for you to enjoy as you go.

Above and left: The Flask is a genteel place to drop in to for refreshment after a hike around Hampstead Heath. The post-war breakdown of class divides allows you to choose whether to patronize the public bar or the saloon bar (pictured).

HOLLY BUSH

◆

ADDRESS: 22 HOLLY MOUNT, NW3
BEERS: HARVEY'S SUSSEX BITTER, ADNAM'S BITTER, FULLER'S LONDON PRIDE
HOURS: MON–SAT 11AM–11PM; SUN 12 NOON–10.30PM

The Holly Bush is one of London's most famous pubs, and many Londoners are likely to have been there at some time or other. Dating back to 1643, the pub was made famous by its association with local residents. The painter George Romney lived and worked next door, and what is now the rear of the pub was formerly his stables, which were incorporated into the pub on his death in 1802. Romney's house was converted into the Hampstead Assembly Rooms, to which the Holly Bush acted as caterer. The pub was, therefore, familiar to an even more famous Hampstead resident, John Constable, who is known to have lectured at the Assembly Rooms in 1836.

The Holly Bush was, however, no stranger to illustrious visitors before Romney and Constable, as James Boswell and Samuel Johnson, Oliver Goldsmith, Leigh Hunt and Charles Lamb are all known to have drunk there. In later years it gained popularity with the stars of music hall; Marie Lloyd was a patron, and, Hampstead being the neighbourhood it is, celebrities from the literary and television worlds can still be seen there on occasion.

The pub has undergone various changes throughout its history. It was one of the last London pubs still to have gas light-ing, and it replaced them only recently. This has altered the character of the front room somewhat, although the fire in the grate is still real. A new snug has been created where the gentlemen's toilets once stood, and to the right of the bar is possibly the smallest snug in any pub anywhere.

Above and below: Most London pub fans have at least heard of, if not visited, Hampstead's Holly Bush, which, until recently, was still gas-lit.

KING'S HEAD

ADDRESS: 115 UPPER STREET, N1

BEERS: TETLEY, BASS, ADNAM'S BITTER, YOUNG'S BITTER, WADWORTH 6X

HOURS: MON–SAT 11AM–11PM; SUN 12 NOON–10.30PM

Not so much a pub as a theatre with a great front of house. The King's Head has been a pub theatre since 1969, before which the auditorium was a boxing ring. It is probably the most famous of London's numerous pub theatres, the largest concentration of which lies in and around Islington (such as the Hen and Chickens and the Old Red Lion, see page 66), as it is one of London's slickest fringe venues and attracts very good productions, many of which go on to greater and more lucrative things.

The theatre motif is unmistakable from the moment you set eyes on the pub, with bills and notices of the current production hanging proud of the pub wall, West End style. Theatre floods provide the lighting beneath a proscenium curtain-like velvet fringe round the bar. One wall is

covered with framed shots from former productions featuring many familiar actors who started out here before hitting the big time. The other wall is given over to details of current and forthcoming productions, as well as lunchtime productions, which the theatre periodically puts on.

There is also a regularly changing programme of live music, though this tends, obviously, to take place after a theatre performance has ended since the auditorium is just to the rear of the pub. The theatre is unusual in that it is possible to get that great London combination of theatre and theatre supper in one place by eating in the auditorium just prior to the show.

Suitably scruffy and admirably determined to go its own way, this pub is to be admired for its eccentricity. Not for them the modern electric till which means that most modern bar staff are now incapable of basic arithmetic. At the King's Head there are still 240 pennies in the pound, as the beautifully ornate antique till is still in service and rings up your order in real, pre-1971 money – pounds that contain 20 shillings, that contain 12 pence – and you will be given the price of your round in old money too!

Above and left: Eccentric and theatrical – in every sense of the word – the King's Head takes on the various roles of pub, restaurant and front of house.

THE MAGDALA

ADDRESS: SOUTH HILL PARK, N3
BEERS: FULLER'S LONDON PRIDE, GREENE KING IPA, GREENE KING ABBOT ALE
HOURS: MON–SAT 11AM–11PM; SUN 12 NOON–10.30PM

Many bloody acts of violence have taken place in London pubs: Christopher Marlowe was stabbed in the eye in a Deptford tavern; a guards officer was thrashed to death in The Grenadier (see pages 84–85); pirates were hanged at Wapping's Prospect of Whitby and two tides allowed to wash over their corpses. All these gruesome acts belong to an unworryingly distant era. However, two pubs in London are associated with murder in living memory. The first is The Blind Beggar on the Mile End Road where East End gangster Ronnie Kray shot dead small-time crook George Cornell; the second was the scene of a tragic crime of passion that went on to become a cause célèbre and create legal history – it is, of course, The Magdala.

On the evening of Easter Sunday 1955, Ruth Ellis waited for her violent and faithless lover David Blakely to leave the pub that sits on the slopes of Parliament Hill. On Blakely's exit Ellis emptied all six rounds from a service revolver at him, five of which hit their target. The sixth bullet ricocheted off the pavement injuring a passerby. For this crime Ruth Ellis's life was terminated at 9am on 18 July 1955 by the famous dynastic hangman Albert Pierrepoint, making her the last woman to be executed by the English courts.

The Ellis case was instrumental in further turning public opinion against the death penalty, and after this and other famous executions which took place against a background of increasing public unease – notably those of 19-year-old Derek Bentley in 1953 and James Hanratty in 1962 – a private members' bill to remove the death penalty for murder from the statute book received Royal Assent on 28 October 1965. Today it remains in place only for acts of treason and piracy with violence.

The Magdala allegedly bears the scars of Blakely's murder – marks visible on the tiles outside the pub are said to have been caused by the bullets. Details of the Ellis case are displayed discreetly inside the rear bar which is largely untouched since that time, though the front bar has been greatly remodelled and is now a pleasant oasis in south Hampstead. In 1984 the Ellis case was turned into a motion picture – *Dance With a Stranger* – starring Miranda Richardson and Ian Holm.

Below: This seemingly unassuming and quiet pub earned its place in London's history books for being the scene of a notorious murder, but is now better known for its excellent food.

O'REILLY'S

ADDRESS: KENTISH TOWN ROAD, NW5

BEERS: NO REAL ALES

HOURS: MON–SAT 11AM–11PM; SUN 12 NOON–10.30PM

The merits and drawbacks of the Irish pub in London are discussed elsewhere (see Quinn's, page 104), but mindful of the caveats expressed there, we offer O'Reilly's as a genuine, kosher, blarney bar for two simple reasons. First, it does it rather well; second, the sheer scale and impact of the Irish diaspora means that you cannot ignore the Irish contribution to the drinking culture of a city like London without selling yourself short. O'Reilly's is, therefore, a place to consider the Irish in London without a green plastic shamrock in sight.

Even cutting through the envious amounts of baloney the Irish construct about themselves, it is undeniable that wit, literature and drink do seem to go together. Not many of the world's great writers were stay-at-home types – the number of pubs in this book alone with which Charles Dickens was demonstrably familiar testifies to that – and when it comes to literature the Irish, for a nation of their size, are without peer.

O'Reilly's challenges your general knowledge with an impressive photographic collection of famous Irishmen. You can have Oscar Wilde and William Butler Yeats as a starter for nothing, but if you are going to get anything close to full marks you will need a decent amount of Irish blood running through your veins.

O'Reilly's may be no more or less authentic than the many Irish pubs in Kilburn, the neighbourhood generally regarded as London's most established Irish quarter, but it certainly lacks the political edge that many Kilburn pubs possess. It is actually quite in order for there to be an Irish population in Kentish Town, for the origin of the name has nothing to do with the eponymous county and everything to do with the Celtic. 'Ken' is Celtic for both 'green' and 'river', and the name Kentish Town – formerly Kentystone – probably meant Green River, since the Fleet, as in Fleet Street, flowed through the original Norman settlement. This etymology is appealing if you consider that it may also apply to Kenwood in Hampstead, with its Iveagh connections – Iveagh being the aristocratic name adopted by the ennobled and enriched descendants of Arthur Guinness, founder of the famous Irish brewery in 1759.

Above left and left: The traditional Irish pub is quite different to its English counterpart, and a trip to O'Reilly's will provide an authentic experience not attainable at the numerous poor imitations that pervade Britain's high streets.

THE PINEAPPLE

◆

ADDRESS: 51 LEVERTON STREET, NW5
BEERS: FULLER'S LONDON PRIDE, MARSTON'S PEDIGREE, BASS
HOURS: MON–SAT 12 NOON–11PM; SUN 12 NOON–10.30PM

Just round the corner from The Assembly House (see page 96) lies a more modest but much-loved local boozer of great character, The Pineapple. During the writing of this book the author's father asked, over the course of a pint in The Fox & Anchor (see page 55), what was the difference between a pub and a bar. One could try and frame a response around a definition of a pub, but since such a definition is notoriously elusive it is a wiser course of action to opt for the reply given: 'If you have to ask, it's a bar.'

I mention this because many people – including, sadly, some in the pub trade – have a very fixed idea of what a pub is, and the premises they have in mind usually have the word 'traditional' painted on the outside. However, there is really no such thing as a traditional pub. Pubs are traditional because, oft times past, people have habitually used them and continue to do so. It is not the pub that is traditional, it is what it does and what people want from it that is.

In London the vast majority of pubs date from the 1890s, whatever the date of the fabric of the building. The term 'pub' did not come into usage until the mid-19th century and was then used to describe improved business premises selling beer that were attempting to distinguish themselves from the gin palaces of the 1820s and 1830s. Prior to this most retail outlets for beer were alehouses, which were very basic affairs, often little more than the front parlour of a private dwelling. The term 'public house', which arose from the recognition that alehouses were primarily private dwellings, did not come into popular usage until most alehouses had been transformed into primarily commercial premises.

The Pineapple, which reopened on 18 May 2002 after refurbishment, is successfully fulfilling a traditional function in a contemporary style. The pub was originally built in 1868, and is now a Grade II listed building as a consequence of its many unusual pineapple motifs and because of a vocal local campaign to 'save The Pineapple', after the widow of the former occupant sold the property to developers for conversion into flats.

Pineapple regulars and local celebrities, such as actors Rufus Sewell and Ken Stott, newscaster Jon Snow and even London Mayor Ken Livingstone became involved in the campaign. Listing the building scuppered the developers' plans and it was sold on to the new owners, who want to keep this handsome and wonderful backstreet pub open to supply the goods, services and functions that The Pineapple and countless pubs like it have traditionally provided.

Below: Pubs can arouse passion – thankfully, as it was the people who felt passionately about The Pineapple who saved this great local pub.

QUINN'S

ADDRESS: 65 KENTISH TOWN ROAD, N1
BEERS: FULLER'S LONDON PRIDE, CHARLES WELLS BOMBARDIER, GREENE KING IPA, GREENE KING ABBOT ALE
HOURS: MON–WEDS 11AM–11PM; THURS–SAT 11AM–2AM; SUN 12 NOON–10.30PM

A fine example of a modern treatment of an older interior, which works because it has been done with attention to detail by people who care. Quinn's is an Irish pub of the best kind. London is full of Irish pubs, most of which owe no more connection to Ireland than they do to Antarctica. 'Plastic Paddy' pubs are easily recognizable because they scream a faux Irishness at you. They are also conspicuous because Irish people studiously avoid them. Quinn's is Irish because the Quinns – who have run the pub with their three sons for 15 years – are Irish (as are many of the world's great publicans), and they bring their love of the trade to the bar.

The pub dates from the early 1800s, though under the Quinns' stewardship it doubled in floor space in 1991 and was further altered in 2001. The centrepiece of the pub is the 15-metre long bar and beautifully carved and illuminated back bar. On the opposite wall the windows are painted with a crude but fun series of tableaux of Edwardian dining-room and drawing-room scenes. These, combined with a sprinkling of various Art Nouveau devices, lends the place a slightly Belgian feel. As luck would have it, Quinn's does a fine range of Belgian beers, as well as a selection of bottled beers from Germany and France – the list runs to around 70 beers; there is a considerable draught range too, more than enough to satisfy the most pernickety connoisseur as well as to whet the appetite of the new initiate. This means that Quinn's has a much wider than average range of beers on offer.

Quinn's is just outside the main catchment area of Camden Market but is well worth the short extra walk, and it is near enough to the Regent's Canal to access all the delights that lie on its banks.

Below left and below: Quinn's is a large, colourful, family-run pub, and a fantastic example of what a pub can be when it is run with a light heart and a dedication to brewing – both British and Belgian.

THE SPANIARDS INN

◆

ADDRESS: SPANIARDS ROAD, NW3
BEERS: ADNAM'S BITTER, FULLER'S LONDON PRIDE, BASS
HOURS: MON–SAT 11AM–11PM; SUN 12 NOON–10.30PM

The Spaniards Inn is one of London's most famous pubs, and this means that it is very much on the tourist trail but still very much worth a visit. As much remains unknown about the pub as is known. There are about as many theories as to the origin of the name as there are authorities on the subject. Some say it is named after a Spanish ambassador to James I's court, who used it as a refuge from a summer plague ravaging London. Others claim that it was named after a Spanish landlord named Francisco Perrero. Yet even more believe that it took its name from two Spanish brothers who once ran it, and the complicated pronunciations of their name led to it being called just The Spaniards. There are even those who maintain that these two brothers once fought a duel over a lady, which led to the demise of one.

Dick Turpin the highwayman was certainly associated with the pub, though do take what you hear of him with a large pinch of salt. He is said to have been born in The Spaniards, but there is equally strong evidence to suggest that he was born in The Crown in Hempstead, Essex. Certainly Essex was very much his patch (see The Black Lion, page 52), and much of the Turpin legend is just that – legend. What *is* known about Turpin is that he was a viscious lout who certainly never deserved any kind of posthumous celebrity, and his famous ride to York almost certainly never took place in the fashion related. Ironically, when arrested in York in 1739, he was using the alias John Palmer, which was the name of the Bath theatre manager who went on in 1784 to found the Royal Mail coaches specifically to contend with the likes of Turpin.

At The Spaniards you will also hear of its role in foiling the Gordon Rioters intent upon destroying the house (now Kenwood House) of Lord Mansfield in 1780. Mansfield had infuriated the anti-Catholic mob and it was only the action of the landlord in throwing open The Spaniards' cellars, so causing the rioters to forget the task in hand for long enough for the militia to arrive and spoil their fun, that prevented the destruction of the mansion.

It remains, therefore, only to say that the list of wits and wordsmiths familiar with The Spaniards is very long. Charles Dickens famously used it as the location for Mrs Bardell's tea party in *The Pickwick Papers*, and Bram Stoker also used it in the darker work *Dracula*.

Left: Be prepared to take the stories that surround The Spaniards Inn with a pinch of salt. Truth need not always crowd out romance, though, and The Spaniards is undoubtedly a very romantic pub.

THE WASHINGTON

ADDRESS: 50 ENGLAND'S LANE, NW3
BEERS: BURTON PA, BASS, GREENE KING IPA, ADNAM'S BITTER, FULLER'S LONDON PRIDE
HOURS: MON–SAT 12 NOON–11PM; SUN 12 NOON–10.30PM

A modern, food-oriented pub set in Victorian surroundings, The Washington must surely be unsurpassed – in North London certainly – in terms of the sheer number of original fittings.

Walking up Primrose Hill Road one is met by George Washington winking at you with an enigmatic smile. The plainness of the inn sign and frontage disguises the feast of finery that hits you when you enter. So sit down at any of the rough tables provided (one is even an old butcher's block) or cosy up on a sofa and prepare to spend a goodly while taking in all the detail.

Look at the varying styles running through the glass panels, mirrors and wood panelling. Are there two eras represented here, or even three? You should admire the mirrors at the rear of the pub on the left side, both astonishingly rare survivals of mid-Victorian high taste, and exceptionally well preserved ones at that (see The Alma, page 126, and The Hope, page 61, for comparisons), with exquisitely painted birds and wild flowers in enamel.

Observe the shape of the bar counter, which blends in beautifully with the moulded wood panelling, and see if you can guess where the missing partition would have been that once divided the pub into three. One partition, or part thereof, remains, and creates a more intimate and secluded area to the rear, popular with those of the canoodling persuasion.

You can also admire the wood carving around the mirrors, which bears such classic legends as 'Champagnes of Noted Brands in Stock', or 'Old Ports and Sherries of the Choicest Vintages'.

There is much more to enjoy than is outlined here, and the pub's current stewards have managed to create a very pleasant modern ambience in the space without in any way detracting from what was there already.

Above and below: A rich abundance of high-Victorian craftsmanship sets The Washington apart from its neighbours in Primrose Hill.

THE WENLOCK ARMS

ADDRESS: 26 WENLOCK ROAD, N1
BEERS: ADNAM'S BITTER, GUEST ALES
HOURS: MON–SAT 12 NOON–11PM; SUN 12 NOON–10.30PM

The Wenlock Arms is a destination pub in a quiet corner of London, just at the edge of the City but without sharing the City's wealth and just on the edge of Islington without sharing Islington's designer chic. It is in a rather forlorn locality that is a mix of houses, light industry and warehouses that would once have taken their trade from the large City Road and Wenlock basins on the Regent's Canal.

It is unlikely that even in its heyday The Wenlock ever attained the fame that it enjoys today, for it is north London's premier real-ale house bar none. Hugely popular with real-ale lovers it serves a terrific range of regularly changing ales and at any one time an impressive number are on tap. Given that the beer choice available in London is limited compared to every other kind of epicurean choice on offer in this most culinary capital, The Wenlock is something of a champion in the eyes of many Londoners. The clientele are a knowledgeable crowd, and will be only too happy to talk you through the full range of ales and beer styles on offer should you need advice.

Ale is not the pub's only attraction, however. It is also a music pub of repute. Sunday lunchtimes is the slot for Colonel Johnny Parker, who can make a piano do just about anything short of sit up and beg. There is a regular traditional jazz band on a Friday night, and the first Saturday of the month is blues night.

The pub, with its handsome central stillion, surrounded by an impressive array of highly eclectic beer bottles – all empty, naturally – features a large blackboard displaying not only the beers currently available, but, importantly for bringing customers back again, the beers that are currently acquiring condition in the cellar and which will be served in the near future.

Left: Yet another notoriously difficult-to-find pub, but as The Wenlock Arms is one of London's finest alehouses persistence pays off.

YE OLDE WHITE BEAR

ADDRESS: NEW END, NW3
BEERS: YOUNG'S BITTER, ADNAM'S BITTER, FULLER'S LONDON PRIDE, GREENE KING ABBOT ALE
HOURS: MON–SAT 11AM–11PM; SUN 12 NOON–10.30PM

Ye Olde White Bear must rate as the best locals' pub in Hampstead, but it does not shout about it. The landlord explains that 'we have several famous patrons but they enjoy their privacy here'. It has also been used on occasion as a television location.

The pub dates back to 1704, and although the present building is Victorian it actually has a rather Georgian feel to it as a result of the interplay of the proportions of the building, the sash windows and the wood panelling on the walls.

A busy back bar creates the necessary feel of clutter and activity. The larger and most handsome of the two main drinking areas is a mass of prints and panels which works very well. The mantelpiece is of a Victorian drawing-room style, surrounded by numerous prints of 'ancestors' all busy reinforcing the impression that smiling was regarded as the height of decadence, and not done by respectable people. Also adorning the walls are signed publicity stills donated by several of the aforementioned famous patrons.

The pub benefits from being a little off the main drag, making it a pleasant house from which to venture forth and enjoy Hampstead Heath, a concert at Kenwood or Kenwood House itself without having to share your refreshment with the hoi polloi. All in all, a rewarding 'find' which, as one reviewer put it, manages, despite its name, to stay on the right side of tweeness. If you really want to enter into the spirit of the pub turn up on a Thursday night and join in the quiz.

Above and below: It may resemble an olde world country pub from the outside, but from the inside Ye Olde White Bear is more like a Victorian drawing room.

WEST LONDON

West London's pubs abound with wisteria and whimsy, but are also wonderfully diverse. Some, such as The White Horse in Fulham, are old country pubs that have seen a city grow up around them, while others, including The Tabard, were built as and when the surrounding streets emerged. There is a wealth of delights to uncover, be it as you meander along the River Thames in the footsteps of England's great designer and writer William Morris (1834–96) or as you pound the pavements along the King's Road in search of a place to quench your thirst after a hard day's shopping for the latest fashions.

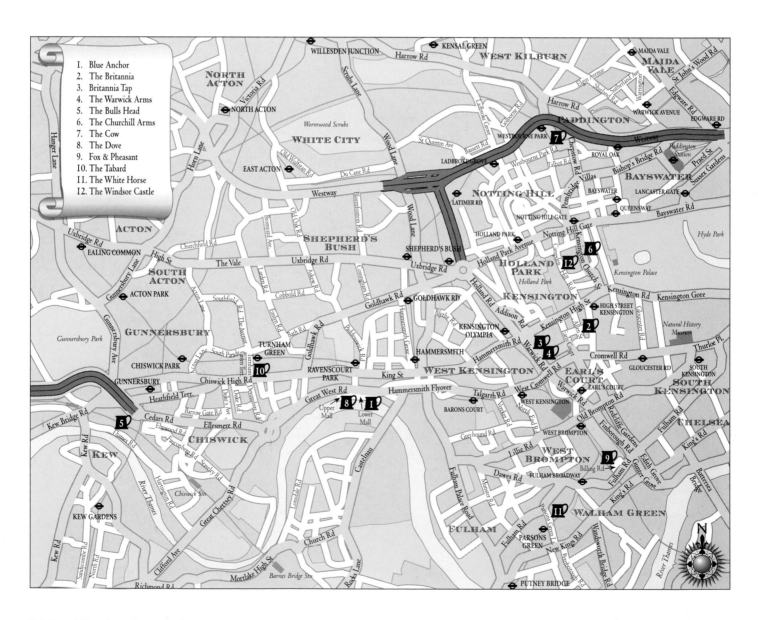

1. Blue Anchor
2. The Britannia
3. Britannia Tap
4. The Warwick Arms
5. The Bulls Head
6. The Churchill Arms
7. The Cow
8. The Dove
9. Fox & Pheasant
10. The Tabard
11. The White Horse
12. The Windsor Castle

BLUE ANCHOR

◆

ADDRESS: 13 LOWER MALL, W6
BEERS: COURAGE BEST, GUEST ALES
HOURS: MON–SAT 11AM–11PM; SUN 12 NOON–10.30PM

As one would expect of a riverside pub situated between the Oxford and Cambridge Boat Race start by Putney Bridge and the race's finish at Mortlake, the Blue Anchor is a rowing pub. It is also a smallish pub, which maximizes its seating area with benches outside on Lower Mall. You are informed as you enter that this tile-fronted building has been licensed since 1722 and that Gustav Holst (who was director of music at St Paul's Girls' School in nearby Brook Green) wrote the Hammersmith Suite here. It is unlikely that the pub has changed much since Holst's day.

Inside, the Blue Anchor has the feel of a rowing clubhouse: blades and oars hang from the ceiling of the wood-panelled interior. Its rowing atmosphere led to its use as a location in the film *Sliding Doors* starring John Hannah, who played a rower, and Gwyneth Paltrow. Walls are adorned with an eclectic range of prints, though the work of local photographer Scott Thompson predominates. Pride of place goes to an antique beer engine, still in working order and very rare (see The Nags Head, page 86, for another example).

Naturally, the pub affords a superb view of the river. St Paul's Boys' School is visible through the trees and to the left is Hammersmith Bridge. The original bridge was the first suspension bridge over the Thames and was built in 1824–27. It was replaced in 1883–87 by Sir Joseph Bazalgette and is now the handsomest river crossing along the Thames.

Heading west it is possible to enjoy a riverside walk that takes you past the Fuller's Brewery in Chiswick, one of the two remaining big London brewery firms (the other being Young's; there is an even larger brewery in Mortlake, but as it only produces the American brand Budweiser it does not count). From there you can walk on to Chiswick House, home of Lord Burlington of Royal Academy fame, and William Hogarth's house, which, ironically, is hard against the wall of Burlington's estate: Hogarth loathed Burlington's Palladian tastes for being very un-English. Over Hammersmith Bridge is the Wetlands Centre, an exceptional wildlife reserve in central London.

Below: Although tables sprawl outside, inside is far more intimate, a feeling only enhanced by the abundance of wood and the print-covered walls.

Previous page: The Blue Anchor's location makes it an ideal starting or finishing point for a walk along the north bank of the River Thames.

THE BRITANNIA

◆

ADDRESS: I ALLEN STREET, W8
BEERS: YOUNG'S BITTER, YOUNG'S SPECIAL, YOUNG'S TRIPLE A
HOURS: MON–SAT IIAM–IIPM; SUN 12 NOON–10.30PM

Kensington is both an ancient settlement and a young part of London. Recorded in the Domesday Book of 1086 as Chenesit, the region just to the north of Kensington High Street from The Britannia has been a settlement ever since. At one time a manor of the Earls of Oxford, in the 17th century it became a popular place for the aristocracy to build large mansions as it offered all the advantages of a country seat within easy reach of London. The area received the royal imprimatur in 1689 when William III commissioned Sir Christopher Wren and others to convert Nottingham House into Kensington Palace.

Kensington has, therefore, always been a wealthy area, and, ever since the Temperance campaigns of the 19th century effectively divorced pubs from upper- and middle-class patronage, pubs in rich neighbourhoods were increasingly to be found in the backstreets for the exclusive use of tradesmen and servants.

The Britannia sits on Allen Street, which was named after a tailor, Thomas Allen, who made a fortune supplying military uniforms during the Napoleonic wars and then turned his hand to property development in the area – although not in Allen Street itself, which stayed as garden ground until around 1893. The area was also home to the Britannia Brewery, and the Allen Street pub was one of only two tied pubs this unsuccessful firm ever managed to secure, the other being The Britannia Tap in Warwick Road (see pages 114–15). The firm went bankrupt in 1902,

and was rescued only to collapse again in 1924 when it was bought out by Young's. The pub was originally known as The Britannia Brewery Tap, shortening its name only in 1938. The present building dates back to 1834, although it was remodelled in 1959–60.

The walls of most London pubs are worthy of inspection, but the prints on display at The Britannia are of a superior quality altogether, with a fair sprinkling of Gillrays and Rowlandsons for the aficionados, and a few H. M. Batemans in the conservatory. Kensington High Street is very much dedicated to shoppers, but there are other attractions too. At Earls Court lies the Commonwealth Institute and on Kensington Gore – which takes its name from the old English 'gara', a triangular piece of land left when ploughing irregularly shaped fields – are the Albert Memorial and Royal Albert Hall.

Above and below: The Britannia is a deceptively large pub, with an exceptional collection of political and satirical cartoons.

BRITANNIA TAP & THE WARWICK ARMS

ADDRESSES: 150 & 160 WARWICK ROAD, W14

BRITANNIA TAP BEERS: YOUNG'S ORDINARY, YOUNG'S SPECIAL, YOUNG'S TRIPLE A, YOUNG'S WAGGLEDANCE

THE WARWICK ARMS BEERS: FULLER'S CHISWICK BITTER, FULLER'S LONDON PRIDE, FULLER'S ESB

HOURS: MON–SAT 12 NOON–11PM; SUN 12 NOON–10.30PM

The beerage is no more. Names that were once synonymous with brewing for generations are now just receding memories. All that is left of Watney's is an American-owned brewery in Mortlake; Courage is now brewed in Newcastle; the once mighty Bass is now Coors; Whitbread stopped brewing in 2001 and has gone the way of other London names: Mann, Crossman, Paulin, Truman, Charrington; only Fuller's and Young's remain. Thankfully there is no great rivalry between the two firms. Traditionally, Young's heartlands were south London and Wandsworth, where its brewery occupies a site that has seen brewing continuously since 1675. Fuller's – the larger firm – has its home across the river in Chiswick and has a reputation for casting its net a little wider.

Rarely do these two brewing giants come up against each other absolutely head to head. One exception, however, is to be found in Warwick Road, between the Earls Court and Olympia exhibition centres. Young's are represented by the Britannia Tap, a narrow, one-room pub, decked out in typically Young's colours – ochre and tan – and with an oasis-like walled garden to the rear. Built as a house in 1823 it later became a beer shop, and in 1905 it was described as a brewery stores and beer house. The Britannia Tap once claimed to be the smallest pub in London – not the only one to have done so – but was enlarged to cope with demand in 1969. Fuller's representative on the streets, The Warwick Arms, is much more in the Fuller's style, with the darker colours – red and green – of Fuller's livery.

One of the reasons that these two family-run firms are content to rub along seemingly oblivious of each other is that their customers are peculiarly partisan. Beer-drinking

Left and opposite page top: Both pubs are fine examples of two breweries' house styles, and Warwick Road provides a rare example of Fuller's and Young's going head to head.

Londoners tend to divide into two camps, Young's drinkers and Fuller's drinkers. Young's beers are more hoppy, the traditional aromas of Goldings and Fuggles hops coming to the fore, while Fuller's are more full-bodied and fruitier (a well-kept London Pride should have hints of strawberry).

Thankfully, both firms, despite wildly different share structures and management styles, are run by descendants of their founders, and the family members in both firms are totally committed to the values that have sustained them: great beer in great pubs. Both Fuller's and Young's continue to grow from strength to strength, and, given that without them there would be almost no choice left in London, long may they continue.

Below: *The interiors of the Britannia Tap (below) and The Warwick Arms are vastly different. The Young's pub celebrates local history, as usual with plenty of black-and-white photographs gracing the wall, while the Fuller's pub is filled to the brim with traditional pub clutter.*

THE BULLS HEAD

ADDRESS: 15 THAMES ROAD, W4

BEERS: THEAKSTON'S BEST, THEAKSTON'S XB, MORLAND'S OLD SPECKLED HEN

HOURS: MON–SAT 11AM–11PM; SUN 12 NOON–10.30PM

It is fashionable to decry as a terrible cliché the claim that London is a series of villages that happen to have bumped into each other. Nevertheless, the portion of Chiswick known as Strand-on-the-Green, bordering the River Thames, is a perfect example of London village life. It is even unlikely that the residents acknowledge that they are in London, and they probably do not have to either, for the area isolated by the Thames to the south and the A4/M4 to the north is one that the vast majority of Londoners never visit. Hence Strand-on-the-Green is a great retreat for people who want to escape London without the motorway misery this normally entails.

Escape is very much a theme at The Bulls Head. Its most famous customer, Oliver Cromwell, was a regular visitor during the English Civil War (1642–49) as his sister Mary, the Duchess of Fauconberg, was a local resident and benefactor. Betrayed to Royalist troops on one occasion, Cromwell escaped from The Bulls Head by a secret tunnel to Oliver's Eyot, the island in the Thames that sits opposite the inn. This island is the first of a surprisingly large number of islands in the Thames, some of which are inhabited. Visiting the pub today one cannot but feel that the Royalist troops were not especially bright or, more probably, not keen to get wet, because the eyot does seem a rather obvious place to look for a recently flown bird.

Appearances can be deceptive and The Bulls Head is a good example of this truism. The core fabric of the building is some 350 years old, but over the years it has expanded to incorporate adjoining cottages, and successive interior decorators have conspired to make it hard to see the joins. Refurbished most recently in the spring of 2002, the pub is deceptively large, with an abundance of nooks and crannies, all on different levels and all given over to dining, making this a destination pub for Sunday lunches in particular. Work up an appetite with a walk along the riverside, or you could cross the river at Kew Bridge and take in the myriad delights of Kew Gardens. Serious walkers could press on along the north bank to Syon Park.

Left: A popular pub since the English Civil War (1642–49), particularly with those who enjoy hearty meals and walks along the Thames Path.

THE CHURCHILL ARMS

ADDRESS: 119 KENSINGTON CHURCH STREET, W8
BEERS: FULLER'S CHISWICK BITTER, FULLER'S LONDON PRIDE, FULLER'S ESB
HOURS: MON–SAT 11AM–11PM; SUN 12 NOON–10.30PM

One might suspect that the landlord of The Churchill Arms is a little bit potty, since there are no fewer than 101 chamber pots hanging on the ceiling. This is certainly one of London's more oddball pubs, and yet in its eccentricity it is truly endearing. The dominant theme is Sir Winston Churchill – portraits of him abound; books by him and about him can be taken down from the shelves; and there is much to learn about this extraordinary man, who clearly believed that destiny had marked him for greatness at a very early age. Churchill takes centre stage in a pantheon of British prime ministers, from Walpole to Wilson, occupying one wall. Meanwhile, in the other arm of the pub a similar compliment is paid to American presidents, from Washington to Nixon.

The pub is divided into distinct areas. To the left of the bar, complete with original snob screens (which along with the number of doors to the street indicate that the pub was once divided into three areas) is the potty/presidents' area. In front of the bar potties give way to hat boxes. To the right of the bar are prime ministers, pots, lanterns and varied hanging ephemera. There is a further area and food servery hidden behind the chimney brace – this is the baskets and butterflies department; some 1,600 butterflies are carefully mounted and framed.

Finally, there is the conservatory dining area, the walls of which are a riot of colour and whose ceiling is a tangle of trailing tendrils from hundreds of pot plants. Thai food is very much the theme here, and the feeling is one of eating in the jungle. To complete the mêlée there's landlord Gerry O'Brien: his name alone is explanation for the Irish flavour, for those of you scratching your heads trying to recall Churchill's Irish connections.

The pub was originally called The Marlborough after Churchill's ancestor and victor of the Battle of Blenheim. Oddly, no mention of him appears at all now.

Above right and right: This pub in a quiet corner of Kensington is divided into a number of sections, each jammed full of ephemera of frequently bizarre origin.

THE COW

ADDRESS: 89 WESTBOURNE PARK ROAD, W2
BEERS: BRAKSPEAR'S BITTER, FULLER'S LONDON PRIDE, FULLER'S ESB
HOURS: MON–SAT 12 NOON–11PM; SUN 12 NOON–10.30PM

On a bench in The Mayflower, Rotherhithe (see pages 150–51), is a quotation from Charles Dickens to the effect that poverty and oysters always go together. At The Cow in Westbourne Park, which styles itself a 'saloon bar and dining rooms', this is demonstrably untrue. Admittedly, they maintain the old custom of serving oysters with Guinness, and Guinness plays quite a large part in the general décor, but the customers of The Cow are not London's working classes. Oysters were a working-class staple in Dickens time, rather than the luxury they are today. Tons and tons of them would have travelled up the Thames from the Whitstable oyster beds to feed the hungry London poor — who would also have drunk porter as their staple liquid intake and another important source of nutrition. Guinness is more properly a stout, but stout is a type of porter and true porter is barely produced today. Hey presto! Guinness and oysters.

The Cow is owned by Tom Conran, who also owns the Lucky Seven a few doors down. When you enter The Cow you may be a little unsure as to where you are or which suburb of Brussels you have landed in. You can ask for a 'bolleke' of De Koninck or a Hoegaarden, the famous aromatic wheat beer which single-handedly saved this Belgian beer style from oblivion. The ambience is decidedly Belgian: the menus are up on mirrors over the dining area; the emphasis is 'gastronomique', and seafood, which lends the whole place the aroma of lemons, is of prime importance, with an ice bar in pride of place keeping fresh the day's stock of oysters, crab and shellfish.

There is a dining room upstairs and the pub also specializes in Cuban cigars. The Cow's motto is 'Eat heartily and give the house a good name,' which is a pretty Belgian sentiment too. Nearby attractions include the Portobello Road street market, and August Bank Holiday weekend sees the famous Notting Hill Carnival take over the entire neighbourhood. The seating outside The Cow makes an ideal spot from which to watch the party.

Above and left: This characterful dining pub has a strong Belgian feel in its beers and menu. This is blended with a traditional oysters-and-stout theme, which is long forgotten in most pubs.

THE DOVE

◆

ADDRESS: 19 UPPER MALL, W6
BEERS: FULLER'S CHISWICK BITTER, FULLER'S LONDON PRIDE, FULLER'S ESB
HOURS: MON–SAT 11AM–11PM; SUN 12 NOON–10.30PM

What do the composer Khatchaturian, the novelists Graham Greene and Ernest Hemingway, and the actors Richard Burton and Rex Harrison have in common? They have all frequented The Dove. This is one of London's premier taverns and it exudes history from its very timbers. On the north bank of the River Thames the pub is known as The Dove, on the south or Surrey side it is known as The Doves as a result of an error on an inn sign facing the river in the 1860s.

The main claim to fame (although it has been contested) of the otherwise largely forgotten poet James Thomson is that he wrote the old Proms favourite 'Rule, Britannia', and he did this at The Dove. However, he also took a boat from The Dove, caught a chill and died. For a full list of celebrities who have passed some time there consult the mantelpiece over the fire in the front bar, where perhaps a couple of hundred names are listed.

William Morris, the writer and Arts and Crafts designer, lived next door – his house is now a museum. A. P. Herbert used The Dove as a model for The Pigeons in his novel *The Water Gipsies*, and Charles II and Nell Gwyn are said to have enjoyed a drink together here. Royalty that definitely did drink at The Dove includes Queen Victoria's uncle Augustus Frederick, Duke of Sussex, who used to retire to the house next door – No. 17, which was once part of the same property – which he referred to as his 'smoking box'. Here, the duke would sit and contemplate the river and plan strategies for the campaign closest to his heart, the abolition of slavery.

Just to the right of the front door is The Dove's other claim to fame – England's smallest bar. The room measures a mere four feet two inches wide, which is 'snug' by any definition of the word. The pub offers a tremendous view of the river as it turns south towards Mortlake and really does invite you to resume the river walk and think Jerome K. Jerome-type thoughts.

Above right and right: You begin to step back in time as soon as you near The Dove and the narrow flagstone path that approaches it; once inside, try to squeeze into the country's smallest bar.

FOX & PHEASANT

ADDRESS: 1 BILLING ROAD, SW10
BEERS: GREENE KING IPA, GREENE KING ABBOT ALE
HOURS: MON–SAT 11AM–11PM; SUN 12 NOON–10.30PM

The Fox & Pheasant takes its influence from the three delightful Georgian terraces that comprise Billing Street and Billing Terrace. These are notable for their delicate pastel-painted houses which make you wonder how many watercolourists must have set up easel in this little oasis under the shadow of Ken Bates's football club-cum-lifestyle complex at Stamford Bridge, home to Chelsea Football Club.

If your idea of a lifestyle complex is a decent boozer then the Fox & Pheasant is likely to fit the bill. A simple two-bar pub with a clever office-style bar reminiscent of those 'lazy s' shaped lovers' seats that enable you to sit next to but facing your paramour. It enables the public and saloon bars to be separate yet served and overseen by just one member of staff. The public bar, naturally, is the sparser of the two yet tends to be the more popular. It opens out to a walled garden that is a real suntrap, enabling you to relax, soak up the heat and completely forget that you are only in SW10.

If you turn right on entering the pub you will find yourself in the saloon, which has a fairly traditional alehouse interior of half-panelling below nicotine-coloured walls.

The pub is only a few yards off the Fulham Road, which has been a major London thoroughfare since the 15th century, when it was called the King's Highway or the London Road. Famous Fulham Road residents have included the writer Arnold Bennett and textile designer Laura Ashley, though whether they visited the Fox & Pheasant is not known (certainly, Ashley's influence is not in evidence).

Below: This 'country' pub in the heart of Fulham is a haven for football lovers, being only minutes from Stamford Bridge.

THE TABARD

◆

ADDRESS: BATH ROAD, W4
BEERS: ADNAM'S BITTER, TETLEY, MARSTON'S PEDIGREE, GREENE KING IPA
HOURS: MON–SAT 11AM–11PM; SUN 12 NOON–10.30PM

The Arts and Crafts movement of the late 19th century has left a surprisingly small footprint on London, and considering that it coincided with a period of frantic pub building there are surprisingly few Arts and Crafts pubs in London. The Tabard, however, is one such. Built in 1880 by the architect Norman Shaw it forms part of the 24-acre development founded by Jonathan Carr that was to be known as Bedford Park. It was Carr's idea to create a middle-class commuting village, made possible by the opening of Turnham Green tube station in 1869, and Bedford Park became the first of what were known as the 'garden suburbs'.

Carr's ambitions were very much in line with the philosophy of the Arts and Crafts movement, and the area attracted aesthetes and politically minded free thinkers. A tabard, as the inn sign by the painter T. M. Rorke depicts, is the tunic worn by a herald. However, the pub may well take its name from the Tabard Inn made famous by Geoffrey Chaucer in *The Canterbury Tales* which had been demolished by property developers in 1875 despite huge public opposition, and perhaps it was to keep the Chaucerian flag flying that the pub took the name.

The interior is unique, with Arts and Crafts tiles by William de Morgan covering the upper walls of the right-hand bar. These tiles are such a fine example of the movement's style that their counterparts are held by the British Museum. De Morgan was a disciple of the great Arts and Crafts

pioneer and radical socialist William Morris, and Morris's influence is very much in evidence. Further tiles, by the artist Walter Crane, in an avant-garde style that would eventually become Art Nouveau, are on display around the fireplace to the left of the bar. The porch, too, is original and the present occupiers have been careful to ensure that the shape and style of furniture and fittings are sympathetic to the building's distinctive lines.

In line with Bedford Park's artistic origins The Tabard boasts its own theatre, which is accessed from the pub's garden. Bedford Park boasts buildings by a number of famous architects, including E. W. Godwin, C. F. A. Voysey and Maurice Adams. W. B. Yeats's family lived there, and G. K. Chesterton knew it well, too.

Above and below: This superb Arts and Crafts pub is an architectural treasure and a refreshing change from the plentiful Victorian pubs in London.

THE WHITE HORSE

ADDRESS: PARSON'S GREEN LANE, SW6
BEERS: ADNAM'S BROADSIDE, HARVEY'S SUSSEX BITTER, ROOSTER'S YANKEE, TIMOTHY TAYLOR'S LANDLORD,
DRAUGHT BASS, HIGHGATE DARK MILD, GUEST ALES
HOURS: MON–SAT 11AM–12 MIDNIGHT; SUN 12 NOON–10.30PM

In 1981, when Fulham was not quite as popular an area as it is today, a young man starting out on a City career offered to help out a friend who had just become the new landlady at The White Horse. There has been a White Horse on the site since 1688, but the building they were presented with dates from 1894. The two friends found a cellar with a bare earth floor containing three barrels of that once great beer Draught Bass. Sally Cruickshank set out to turn the pub around, Mark Dorber set out to learn about cellarmanship. Over 20 years later, Sally has retired and Mark has long since given up his City job in order to become a successful publican in his own right.

The White Horse prides itself on doing everything well. The kitchen, under the control of Heidi Flett, produces superb food, and has spawned a number of chefs who have gone on to good London restaurants. Each month Mark hosts a gourmet evening at which each dish is carefully matched to a different beer. Championing the cause of beer is very much Dorber's life, and, as well as gourmet evenings, The White Horse is likely to be planning or hosting one of many brewing industry events. It could be the National Hop Association's annual Beauty of Hops Competition or the Wheat Beer Challenge. It runs its own famous Old Ale Festival and quarterly beer festivals, and you never know which of the pub's many friends from breweries of all nations will be in town paying their respects.

In summer the large patio throngs with the new breed of Fulhamites who have colonized and changed the area since the early 1980s, and who have earned the pub the moniker 'The Sloaney Pony'. Old Fulham still exists, however, and makes its presence felt occasionally, especially when Chelsea are playing at home. The White Horse is also home to a vast army of usually foreign youngsters who have absorbed the ethos of high-quality beers, food and service that mark a White Horse graduate from the backpackers who pull pints in hundreds of London pubs and pass on without learning anything. The White Horse ethos has been exported to countless restaurants, hotels and bars worldwide. If ever a pub was an ambassador for a nation it is this one.

Above and left: The White Horse is London's finest real-ale pub, and as such has a truly international reputation — no brewer visits London without paying a visit to this excellent establishment.

THE WINDSOR CASTLE

ADDRESS: 114 CAMPDEN HILL ROAD, W11
BEERS: FULLER'S LONDON PRIDE, ADNAM'S BITTER, BASS
HOURS: MON–SAT 12 NOON–11PM; SUN 12 NOON–10.30PM

It is unlikely that there is any truth in the story that The Windsor Castle got its name because on a clear day it was possible to see Windsor Castle from Campden Hill. However, once inside the pub, looking out of the window is likely to be fairly low down your 'to do' list, as this magnificent early Victorian boozer is a real feast for the eyes.

The Windsor Castle must contain one of the least altered Victorian interiors in London. It is still partitioned by fairly solid wood screens, into which are set tiny interconnecting doors. These doors were intended for use by bar staff and cleaners and not customers, which is why they were discreetly small. Customers were expected to exit the pub and re-enter by another door if they wished to change drinking area. (Today, only the Prince Alfred in Maida Vale can boast similar features, but this has recently been turned into a bistro so no longer really counts as a pub. Hopefully one day someone will realize its origins and restore it to its proper status and glory.)

Each of the doors into The Windsor Castle bears its own legend. There is the Campden Bar, the Private Bar and, intriguingly, the Sherry Bar. The latter is a reference to the pub's sadly extinct tradition of serving a drink called the Hunter, which is a bit like a Bloody Mary but with sherry rather than vodka.

Beautifully dingy, The Windsor Castle has lots of original dark wood, settles and rustic benches, and the nicotine-stained walls only add to the warm feeling that would have been so important in attracting custom in the days when escaping the cold was of rather more significance than it is today. In warmer weather, a pleasant garden area is also open.

The pub is also well known for its range of sausages, as well as the house specialities of mussels and oysters. It is within easy walking distance of Portobello Road Market, Kensington Gardens and Holland Park.

Below: This old alehouse has the air of the countryside about it, but sits in the heart of fashionable Kensington.

SOUTH-WEST LONDON

South-west London is the fiefdom of those most admirable of fellows, Young's.
There has been a brewery in Wandsworth since 1581, so it is not surprising that Young's
have managed to claim the region as their own. Fortunately, given Young's unfashionably
dogged determination to do things the traditional way – including delivering beer by
horse-drawn dray – south-west London is a particularly rich treasure trove of delightful
public houses. Right from the first entry in this chapter, The Alma in Wandsworth,
through to the last, Ye White Hart in Barnes, you will be assured of a perfect pint of bitter
whichever Young's establishment you choose to patronize. However, Young's do not always
have it their own way, and there are enough superb non-Young's pubs south of the river,
including Stockwell's Priory Arms and Battersea's Woodman, to ensure that the chaps
from Wandsworth are kept on their toes.

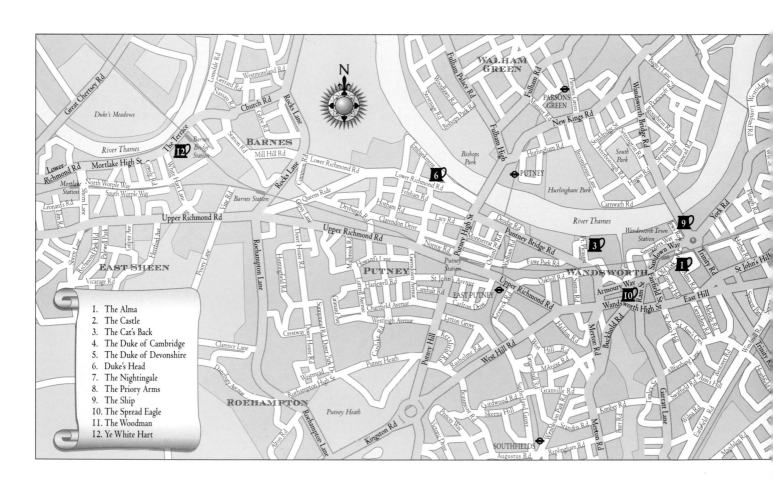

1. The Alma
2. The Castle
3. The Cat's Back
4. The Duke of Cambridge
5. The Duke of Devonshire
6. Duke's Head
7. The Nightingale
8. The Priory Arms
9. The Ship
10. The Spread Eagle
11. The Woodman
12. Ye White Hart

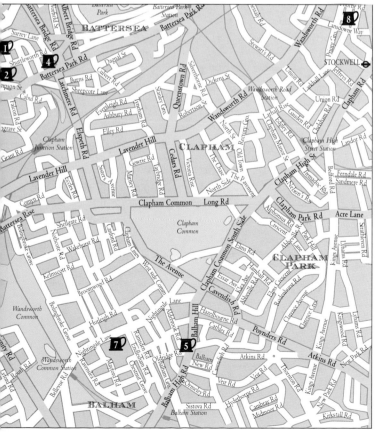

THE ALMA

ADDRESS: 499 OLD YORK ROAD, SW18
BEERS: YOUNG'S BITTER, YOUNG'S ORDINARY, YOUNG'S TRIPLE A
HOURS: MON–SAT 11AM–11PM; SUN 12 NOON–10.30PM

On the outside The Alma is an inspiring and handsome mid-Victorian London pub, on the inside a French fin-de-siècle bistro. Built in 1866, it takes its name from nearby Alma Road and Alma Cottages, which were built around 1854 at the time of the Battle of the Alma in the Crimean War.

The big open lounge room is a mix of features and styles. The origin of the chairs is not in doubt – they have obviously been salvaged from churches, while the large central bar is a hotchpotch of many styles. On the walls are three unique mosaic roundels featuring the pub's name. The corner area around the broad wooden stairs is beautifully decorated with painted mirrors, which are just right for the period (mid-19th centruy) and extremely rare. Further mirrors in the little alcove under the stairs are reminiscent of other fine examples found in The Washington (see page 107) in Primrose Hill. The gallic feel of the pub is accentuated by the choice of furniture, an old cool box, a picture of a French village square, and painted tables.

To the rear is a dining room serving good-quality modern pub cooking. Here the main feature is a rustic table of immense proportions, and the room also boasts a decorative plaster frieze that had previously been hidden and was only discovered during renovation in 1987.

Being some 200 yards from the back of Young's Brewery, this – like pretty much every pub in SW18 – is naturally a Young's house, serving the brewery's widely respected ales. Young's itself is a major attraction in the area, and tours of the brewery are frequent, very comprehensive and end in their famous sampling room. In the unlikely event that their ales are not to your taste, Young's is also one of the few regional breweries to brew its own lager, which is commonly regarded as rather good compared with the generally poor-quality lagers brewed in the UK.

The tour will also take you round the stables to the rear of the brewery. Young's is now the only brewery still to use horses in a working capacity, delivering beer daily to pubs within a three-mile radius.

Below: The central bar is now the main focus in this redesigned Victorian pub, where an eclectic collection of furniture and brightly painted tables create a cheerful, relaxed atmosphere.

Previous pages: The vast conservatory at the back of The Ship (top) is a lovely setting for a pub lunch beside the River Thames at Wandsworth. In comparison, The Nightingale (bottom) is surrounded by the leafy residential streets of Balham, but is nonetheless welcoming and very cosy.

THE CASTLE

ADDRESS: 115 BATTERSEA HIGH STREET, SW11
BEERS: YOUNG'S BITTER, YOUNG'S SPECIAL, YOUNG'S TRIPLE A
HOURS: MON–SAT 12 NOON–11PM; SUN 12 NOON–10.30PM

Lest anyone think the taste for pubs expressed in this book runs too much towards the high Victorian, The Castle should dispel the notion. The taste of this book runs towards greatness and it just happens that one of the tests of greatness is longevity. Similarly what makes a great pub is not the elaborateness of the bricks and mortar but rather the character of the people who occupy it at any time.

With The Castle something special has been created from something nondescript, for it would cause offence in no quarter at all to describe the building that houses The Castle as a first-class example of unspeakably bad 1960s architecture. As a pub, however, it works. This may be down to the fact that there has been – as the foundation stone will tell you – a pub named The Castle on the site since c. 1600, when, aside from being home to Anne Bullen (Boleyn), wife to Henry VIII, this part of old Battersea was mostly marsh and market gardens.

The fabric of the building changed over the years, and in the 18th century it was a coaching inn with a bay window at first-floor height from which passengers could step onto the coach roof. The old Castle was demolished in 1963 to make way for council flats, and during excavations workmen unearthed a pot containing 49 gold sovereigns, 34 half sovereigns and some silver. A sovereign and half sovereign are buried under the foundation stone. The Castle is also the proud owner of its original and very rare Elizabethan carved sign, which was discovered in the 1950s.

Today The Castle is a great food pub while managing to maintain the atmosphere of a traditional pub. The menu changes daily and there is an above average wine list. The space is light and airy, with lots of pot plants, a conservatory and garden. It is a great place to enjoy the Sunday papers.

Above and below: An authentic Elizabethan carved sign sits proudly on the 1960s exterior of this historic pub. The Castle may occupy a relatively modern building but that is just packaging, as ale has been served on this site since the early 17th century.

THE CAT'S BACK

ADDRESS: 86–88 POINT PLEASANT, SW18
BEERS: O'HANLON'S, BLAKELEY'S NO. 1 AND GUEST BEERS
HOURS: MON–SAT 11AM–11PM; SUN 12 NOON–10.30PM

If you have done the Young's thing – the brewery, The Spread Eagle (see page 135), The Ship (see page 134), and The Alma (see page 126) – and perhaps fancy a bit of a contrast or even a complete and utter contrast, you should endeavour not to miss The Cat's Back. This is a great alternative pub of the kind that looks as if it should really be in Camden Market or the Portobello Road.

The Cat's Back is a free house and has been under its present ownership since 1994. Despite being built in 1865, it has a distinct 1950s Bohemian feel to it and a décor that could be described as part antique shop, part house clearance and part theatre props store. The walls are covered in everything from ethnic masks to family photos; you can sit on a throne of the regal rather than lavatorial variety, or on a variety of delightfully hideous plastic chairs. An overly long description of all the delights of The Cat's Back would spoil the enjoyment, save to say that when you walk down Point Pleasant the pub can be spotted from the distinctive petrol bowser outside. For those who stumble across it – which you, having the advantage of a guide, will not have to rely on doing – it is a happy find.

Beers come from the award-winning O'Hanlons Brewery which was formerly in Vauxhall before relocating to Exeter, but which has nevertheless managed to retain the loyalty of its London customers due to the quality of its ales. Your enjoyment of both pub and beer will come with a sound-track of eclectic music which always seems just right for the mood. All in all, The Cat's Back is a study in eccentricity – and where better to be eccentric than in a pub? Those visitors who appreciate the outdoors should be sure to take in nearby Wandsworth Park.

Below: Good music, good beer, free-house status and off-the-wall walls make The Cat's Back stand out from the crowd.

THE DUKE OF CAMBRIDGE

ADDRESS: 228 BATTERSEA BRIDGE ROAD, SW11
BEERS: YOUNG'S BITTER, YOUNG'S SPECIAL, YOUNG'S TRIPLE A
HOURS: MON–SAT 11AM–11PM; SUN 12 NOON–10.30PM

Walking into The Duke of Cambridge is a bit like walking into a David Hockney picture: lots of bold colours and strong lines and an immediately striking impression. The brainchild of Nick Elliot and Joanne Clevely, who cut their teeth at The Chelsea Ram and The Queens in Regent's Park Road, this is an example of how to take an old pub and give it a sympathetically contemporary slant.

One of six Dukes owing fealty to Young's Brewery, this particular establishment was built in the early 1860s when Battersea was rapidly developed as a result of the construction of Battersea Bridge. The pub's stables were once home to a volunteer fire crew in the days before the foundation of the London Fire Brigade. They were also used by the No. 34 omnibus from Islington to Battersea, one of the last horse-drawn buses in London, which, of course, was killed off by the arrival of the railway at Nine Elms in 1838 and Clapham Junction (Britain's busiest railway station) in 1846.

The duke himself, whose photograph adorns a wall, was very much an animal-rights activist. In 1886 he instituted the London Cart Horse Parade in Battersea Park, the objectives of which were – and still are – to improve the general condition and treatment of London's cart horses, to encourage drivers to take a human interest in the animals under their care, and to encourage the wider use of powerful cart horses on London's streets. Between 1888 and 1994 the parade took place in Regent's Park, and in 1995 the London Harness Horse Parade moved back to its original home a few yards from The Duke of Cambridge. Fittingly, the present president of the parade is John Young, Chairman of Young's Brewery, which still uses heavy horses to deliver beer to pubs within a three-mile radius of the brewery. The parade takes place every Easter Monday, and whereas the 1886 parade had 106 entries, the 2002 parade had 206 – no doubt the duke would be pleased.

Much to be admired is the mural to the rear of the pub by the artist Paul Karslake. All the regulars are featured, and the masterful painting required an impressive spatial awareness by the artist, painting a scene both in reverse and from a point of view that he could not see. The daily changing menu makes this a seriously good food pub and the general confidence and ease of touch with which the whole place is run marks it out as first-class.

Below: The style of The Duke of Cambridge is very modern yet full of character and interest; the pub itself dates from Victoria's reign.

THE DUKE OF DEVONSHIRE

ADDRESS: 39 BALHAM HIGH ROAD, SW12
BEERS: YOUNG'S BITTER, YOUNG'S SPECIAL, YOUNG'S TRIPLE A
HOURS: MON–TUES 11AM–11PM; WED–THURS 11AM–12 MIDNIGHT; FRI–SAT 11AM–2AM; SUN 12 NOON–10.30PM

The wheel comes full circle at the fabulous and wonderfully preserved Duke of Devonshire in Balham. Music halls grew out of high-Victorian pubs of this ilk. The walk down this long pub up to the balcony area and the late-night bar is reminiscent of an entrance into one of the concert halls that many south London pubs added as late-night attractions. As these halls became more popular the authorities realized that here was a new form of popular entertainment, and they legislated to split music halls from the consumption of alcohol.

As an interior The Duke of Devonshire must rank in London's top ten, and, given the size of the pub, it is in many respects unsurpassed. A pub of the same name dates back to at least 1827, and for many years it was a beer house only – that is, it didn't have a licence to sell spirits or wine. Beer houses were an attempt to substitute beer consumption (wholesome) for gin consumption (poisonous). Even so it was a very busy house. In 1857 it was doing some 613 butts of porter per annum – that's 1,450 pints a day. In order to serve this volume it's no wonder that the bar at The Duke is so massive. Shaped like a giant G-clamp, it is some 45 yards in length, and behind it is a sumptuous array of etched glass. This is very much in the style that became known as gin palace, though real gin palaces were actually much plainer.

Not all the windows in The Duke are original, but the later ones are still handsome and do not detract from the gin palace style. Sadly, electric light can never recapture the true feel of gas, but it requires no great leap of imagination to recreate the magnificence of The Duke of Devonshire in the muggy days of gas lighting. An interior like this cannot fail to stimulate the mind.

Above and left: The Duke has one of London's 'don't miss' pub interiors – this pub, which is Balham's pride, is opulence embodied. Its modest location on Balham High Road gives little away about the architectural finery that lies within.

DUKE'S HEAD

◆

ADDRESS: 8 LOWER RICHMOND ROAD, SW15
BEERS: YOUNG'S BITTER, YOUNG'S SPECIAL, YOUNG'S TRIPLE A
HOURS: MON–SAT 11AM–11PM; SUN 12 NOON–10.30PM

The original 1832 Duke's Head was rebuilt in 1864 and further altered in 1894, but has always been in the Young's Brewery portfolio. It has the kind of London pub interior that no one would manage to look after quite as well as Young's. The Duke's Head has something for every taste. The lads and locals will congregate in the back bar, furthest from the river, while the main action is on the river side. The principal hustle and bustle takes place in the front dining room, which affords river views on three sides, including the best view of the start of the Oxford and Cambridge Boat Race (this takes place on the first Saturday in April each year, and has done since 1854).

Almost as busy is the area round the elaborate and original bar. Island bars were very much a mid-Victorian innovation and owe their invention to the famous engineer Isambard Kingdom Brunel. Passengers on Brunel's Great Western Railway often faced a short but necessary wait at Swindon, and the railway's bar was too small to serve all the thirsty customers before it was time for the porters to shout 'all aboard' once more. Brunel realized that a round 'island' bar maximized the available bar frontage in relation to the number of people waiting and staff serving, meaning that more people could be served in the same time with less frustration.

pockets plying their trades in obscure pub corners). As a result pubs were forced to reduce the number of rooms they had and many island bars went, literally, to the wall.

Above and below: The Duke's Head is always packed in April for the annual Boat Race, but the pub's good river views from a salon-style setting means that it's pretty busy every other day of the year, too.

The idea caught on and boosted the trend of the 1870s and 1880s for pubs to be divided into an increasing number of rooms and snugs. Privacy soon became the main theme, and, with the improvement in acid-etching techniques, frosted glass and snob screens became the order of the day.

Towards the end of the century licensing magistrates reacted against the increasing complexity of this fashion and favoured greater supervision and all-round visibility (they were paranoid about prostitutes and pick-

THE NIGHTINGALE

ADDRESS: 97 NIGHTINGALE LANE, SW12
BEERS: YOUNG'S BITTER, YOUNG'S SPECIAL, YOUNG'S TRIPLE A
HOURS: MON–SAT 11AM–11PM; SUN 12 NOON–10.30PM

Nightingale Lane was originally known as Balham Wood Lane, and no one is sure whether the pub is named after the lane or the lane after the pub, or whether the truth lies elsewhere — with those who maintain that the area was once noted for nightingales' song.

The pub was built in a deliberately unpub-like style as part of the disposal of the Old Park Estate which was sold in lots in 1869. The estate owners clearly had views on what sort of a neighbourhood should be created by the developers of this previously rural area. For example, they stipulated that no house could be sold for less than £800 and that no house should be within 25 feet of the road.

The Nightingale has been a Young's pub since 1920. Today it is widely respected and is definitely a good, reliable local. It is also a versatile house catering for a number of different types of clientele at different times of day. Lunchtime sees the old boys nursing a leisurely pint but also quite brisk trade from the surprisingly large number of office workers hidden in this ostensibly residential neighbourhood. In the evenings the average age drops slightly as people return from work in central London.

The Nightingale's interior is very much in the Young's style with nicotine-stained walls and rich wood hues, with a relatively low ceiling (by London standards), all interacting to suffuse this single-roomed pub with a cosy welcoming glow.

A good clue to the community nature of The Nightingale are the 32 photographs of guide dogs that the pub has raised money for over the years, and this is a valuable reminder that pubs like The Nightingale are the cornerstone of much charity fundraising all over the country.

Above and left: Whether they be office workers, old boys or locals, The Nightingale's appealing exterior and interior draw in a broad spectrum of Balham and Clapham's populace.

THE PRIORY ARMS

ADDRESS: 83 LANSDOWNE WAY, SW8
BEERS: PRIORY ARMS RANGE
HOURS: MON–SAT 11AM–11PM; SUN 12 NOON–10.30PM

Many books on pubs are produced by people with an interest in beer and beer alone and so tend to reflect that interest. Although this volume has a slightly more varied approach to what makes a good pub excellent, it is only proper that certain pubs will find their way in as a result of their beer-selling activities. A small number of London pubs have a reputation based wholly or partly on the quality or variety of their beers, such as The White Horse, The Greenwich Union and The Wenlock Arms, which are all in this volume; it is only proper that The Priory is too.

By and large London is an appalling place to drink beer, if your idea of good beer really means 'bitter' or 'real ale'. Despite being the national drink of England, ale now sadly constitutes only 10 per cent of all beer consumed. Beer aficionados know that not all beer is good beer in the same way that gourmets know not to dine at a McDonald's just because it styles itself as a restaurant. In The Priory you will discover that there are some stubborn souls who regard beer as every bit the equal of wine.

Some pubs spend a lot on décor to distract one from the fact they actually offer very little that any other pub is not offering. The Priory sells nothing save that which is out of the ordinary and uses that fact as the basis for its decoration. Pump clips from hundreds of beers from Britain's countless unsung independents form the basis of visual relief in this otherwise plainly furnished space. Indeed, The Priory elevates the pump clip to an art form and demonstrates that when it comes to visual wit, flair, skill and style Britain's brewers and pump-clip artists can give the Tate Modern a good run for its money.

Garry Morris, the dynamic creator of The Priory, is proud of the fact that this is a genuine free house (i.e. entirely his business) – a rarity these days, although in times past all pubs were free houses. The Priory demonstrates that a free house under the right owner will always beat a tenanted or managed house.

Below: The Priory Arms is not only south London's leading real-ale pub, but is also, and very proudly, a free house – a rarity in the city.

THE SHIP

◆

ADDRESS: 41 JEWS ROW , SW18
BEERS: YOUNG'S BITTER, YOUNG'S SPECIAL, YOUNG'S TRIPLE A
HOURS: MON–SAT 11AM–11PM; SUN 12 NOON–10.30PM

The sister pub to The Alma (see page 126) – they share the same management team, and even the same loyalty-card scheme – The Ship is in a similar mould but on a grander scale. A riverside pub with a large outdoor area and a great atmosphere, it has views of the river that, although they don't really compare with those from the Duke's Head, are decidedly better than in years gone by when a row of cottages existed between the river and the pub. The brewery bought the cottages in 1848 with the express intent of knocking them down.

The main part of the building, dating back to 1809 and first leased by Young's in 1832, is the least used part – the front bar can be empty while the riverside bar is thronging. The focus of the pub is all in the conservatory, which was added only in 1988. One side is a proper restaurant serving modern British cuisine of a standard that makes it advisable to book.

In recent years a permanent barbecue has been built to serve the outdoor trade, and there is even a summer bar – Doolali – in a beach-bar-type shack to cope with the considerable seasonal trade the pub attracts. The clientele is predominantly young professional, and is likely to remain so given the amount of 'executive' apartment building that has gone on and is set to continue in the neighbourhood.

Riverside walking to the east is not possible, but to the west things are improving, allowing you to take in Wandsworth Park on the way to Putney. Nearby attractions include Young's Brewery, the Hurlingham Club and Bishop's Park.

Left: This gastro pub has a trendy young professional clientele that is attracted to the fine dining, well-kept beers, great beer garden and riverside location offered by The Ship – what more could they ask for?

THE SPREAD EAGLE

ADDRESS: 71 WANDSWORTH HIGH STREET, SW18
BEERS: YOUNG'S BITTER, YOUNG'S SPECIAL, YOUNG'S TRIPLE A
HOURS: MON–SAT 11AM–11PM; SUN 12 NOON–10.30PM

Among the declining band of authentic Victorian pub interiors The Spread Eagle could clearly claim aristocratic status. Grandeur is the word that springs to mind as soon as you enter this large, imposing space, and grandeur was what was in the forefront of the minds of the designers. As you contemplate the sheer extent of the glasswork in the pub you might consider that 'magnificence' would also be a good word at this juncture. The Spread Eagle was certainly thought of as grand by the well-to-do of Wandsworth society in the late 19th century.

The pub was in existence prior to 1780, and by 1836, when it was acquired by Young's, it was already an important coaching inn and therefore very much part of the commercial centre of Wandsworth. Magistrates would meet there and various civic functions took place, including the first meeting of the proprietors of Surrey Iron Railway. It is impressive to consider that The Spread Eagle was considerably more extensive in the mid-19th century than today. The brewery property book of 1857 states that 'these premises occupy a commanding position in the High Street with considerable frontage in Garratt Lane. They consist of a tavern and tea garden, a large ballroom, a portion of which is now used as the County Court, a separate tap which has a licence of its own and a considerable range of stabling.'

In later years and until 1890 the Assembly Rooms on this site were used for music-hall acts and then became one of London's first bioscope cinemas. The 19th-century features visible today date from the complete rebuilding of the pub in 1898, when much of the extra space was disposed of. Young's Brewery is just across the street.

Above and below: The Spread Eagle is a superb example of the grand Victorian pub, complete with fine glasswork and a spacious bar.

THE WOODMAN

ADDRESS: 60 BATTERSEA HIGH STREET, SW11
BEERS: BADGER BEST BITTER, TANGLEFOOT, KING AND BARNES SUSSEX
HOURS: MON–SAT 11AM–11PM; SUN 12 NOON–10.30PM

Mention The Woodman to most south Londoners and they will think of the pub with the table of board games, puzzles and parlour games. Just a few yards from trendy and village-like Battersea Square, this long, narrow Hall and Woodhouse pub was very much a yuppie hangout in the late 1980s. Yuppies have given way to 'dinkies', and a new generation of young couples now fill The Woodman.

The Woodman goes on much as before, both as a good ale boozer and a fun pub. The front area, with its eccentrically shaped island bar, is suitably traditional and opens out to a long extension leading to an enclosed outdoor seating area. This is where you sit and frown in frustration as you attempt one of the games, be it negotiating a ball bearing through a maze while avoiding the traps, pulling one stick from a pile of sticks without disturbing the others, trying to expand the English language with a new seven-consonant word or vainly trying to keep your queen beyond move number five.

The pub was once one of the few London outlets for Hall and Woodhouse favourites such as Badger beer and Tanglefoot, and although these ales can be found in more and more pubs, The Woodman is still very much a promoter of the Dorset brewery.

Live music, fine ales, outdoor barbecues and a general fun atmosphere make this a good all-rounder with commendable cross-generational appeal.

Below: Brewers Hall and Woodhouse ensure that excellent beer is available at the front-of-house island bar, while out back a variety of games are on hand to ensure The Woodman has a relaxed and fun atmosphere.

YE WHITE HART

ADDRESS: THE TERRACE, RIVERSIDE, SW13
BEERS: YOUNG'S BITTER, YOUNG'S SPECIAL, YOUNG'S TRIPLE A
HOURS: MON– SAT 11AM–11PM; SUN 12 NOON–10.30PM

The White Hart is one of London's largest waterside pubs, commanding an impressive sweep of the river at the base of the Barnes reach as it curves northwards again towards Chiswick. It is a popular destination on a sunny day, and with seating on the terrace and below on the towpath it is capable of accommodating several hundred people without appearing crowded. Nevertheless, even Ye White Hart will get crowded on the day of the Oxford and Cambridge Boat Race as it offers one of the best vantage points of the race: unlike the Putney pubs such as the Duke's Head (see page 131), the battle is often still being hard fought as the boats pass beneath the pub towards the finish at The Ship quarter of a mile or so further upstream.

Established in 1662, Ye White Hart is one of the oldest pubs in this part of London. The manor of Mortlake, of which Barnes was then a part, was already a well-established settlement by this time. The first written reference to the inn is from 1676 (it was then known as The King's Arms) when, on the death of Robert Warner, a cooper, it passed to his son Charles. The pub stayed in the Warner family's hands until 1736. In 1766 it was acquired by the Trevy family of neighbouring Putney, who changed the name to Ye White Hart.

It entered the estate of the Wandsworth brewery firm of Young and Bainbridge, as Young's was originally known, in 1857, and towards the end of the 19th century it was extensively rebuilt, which resulted in its current exterior and appearance. The large balconies enabled the pub to capitalize on the bonanza that the Boat Race affords, and this also accounts for the balustrade running round the edge of the uncharacteristically flat roof. Given the presence of the function room on the first floor, Ye White Hart is very much south-west London's answer to the Greenwich taverns that boasted large ballrooms on their upper floors, of which the Trafalgar Tavern (see page 155) is the only survivor.

Above and below: Ye White Hart has impressively spacious premises designed to take full advantage of the views of the River Thames.

SOUTH-EAST LONDON

South-east London is probably the most diverse region in the city – Peckham, for example, sharing few similarities with neighbouring Dulwich. As such, it has a superb variety of pubs, from The Market Porter in the bustling thoroughfares of Borough to The Greenwich Union which sits in genteel backstreets. One regular feature, however, is the River Thames: once the major source of employment for the area's residents, it now forms the backdrop to a large number of the establishments selected here.

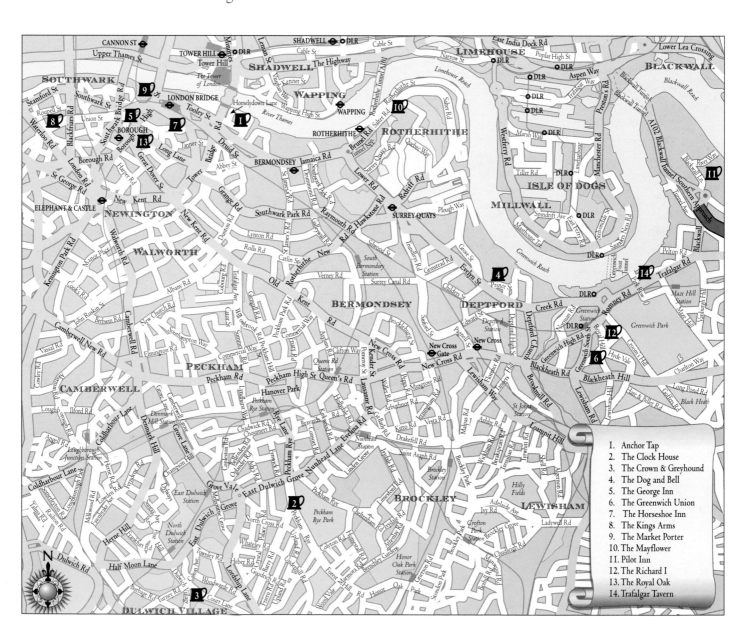

1. Anchor Tap
2. The Clock House
3. The Crown & Greyhound
4. The Dog and Bell
5. The George Inn
6. The Greenwich Union
7. The Horseshoe Inn
8. The Kings Arms
9. The Market Porter
10. The Mayflower
11. Pilot Inn
12. The Richard I
13. The Royal Oak
14. Trafalgar Tavern

ANCHOR TAP

◆

ADDRESS: 20A HORSLEYDOWN LANE, SE1
BEERS: SAM SMITH'S OLD BREWERY BITTER
HOURS: MON–SAT 11AM–11PM; SUN 12 NOON–10.30PM

The Anchor Tap takes its name from the old Anchor Brewery, which, if you are standing on Tower Bridge facing south, is the joyously complicated building squeezed between the bridge and Butler's Wharf. The Anchor was one of many Southwark breweries that clustered along the Thames from the days of Queen Elizabeth I.

Today the Anchor Tap is owned by the Yorkshire brewery firm Sam Smith's of Keighley. The Yorkshiremen are to be greatly admired, for not only do they add an element of choice to London's beer market, but a careful pub-buying policy means that their London estate is of exceptionally high quality, and a large proportion of their pubs are celebrated in this book.

Although Sam Smith's owns fewer pubs than the two remaining London brewers, Young's and Fuller's, ounce for ounce the average Sam Smith's pub weighs several carats more than its rivals. As if this were not enough they also sell their beers considerably below normal London prices, despite having to ship it some 150 miles further than their London counterparts. This is due to the fact that Sam Smith's is one of those rare creatures – an unlimited company. There are only a handful of these, and shareholders have unlimited liability for company debts, but on the plus side the company's affairs are entirely transparent and the directors can do very much as they please without having markets or accountants tell them otherwise.

Sam Smith's unusual financial status has made a major contribution to the preservation of a significant number of important London buildings that would have been unlikely to fare so well under limited or public company ownership; the Anchor Tap is one of these. Frugal and uncluttered, the pub is reminiscent of the days when its customers were warehousemen, dockers and sailors. It actually has quite a northern feel to it, though this is by no means a feature of Sam Smith's London estate – quite the contrary. The Anchor Tap certainly benefits from being the best pub for quite a way in any direction, so bear this in mind when planning your day if you are thinking of visiting HMS *Belfast*, the Design Museum, Bermondsey Antiques Market or any of Southwark's other attractions.

Left: The Anchor Tap's unique atmosphere brings a touch of Yorkshire to the banks of the Thames.

Previous page: The Pilot Inn is a great local pub that has refused to let anything, even the nearby Millennium Dome, stop it from serving.

THE CLOCK HOUSE

ADDRESS: 196A PECKHAM RYE, SE19
BEERS: YOUNG'S BITTER, YOUNG'S SPECIAL, YOUNG'S TRIPLE A
HOURS: MON–SAT 11AM–11PM; SUN 12 NOON–10.30PM

If you walk south along Peckham Rye you stumble across The Clock House quite by chance, as it is tucked round the bend in the road created by the junction of Peckham Rye and Barry Road. The suddenness with which you come across it adds to the joy of discovering just how charming a pub it is. A front patio is fronted by a trellis on which ivy is working inwards from the southern end and a wisteria is creeping up from the north.

Originally a Victorian shop and then an off-licence, The Clock House was purchased by Young's in 1962, though it was not until 1969 that a full on-licence was obtained and the conversion into a pub undertaken. The off-licence name was retained – it derived from the Victorian clock that sits under the gables – and this provided the inspiration for the décor. Clocks are very much a theme – big clocks, that is. Several are dotted round the pub, and some even tell the correct time.

The whole pub is decorated in a tasteful dark green. An old inn sign takes pride of place over the bar, while above the main space is a delightfully ornate chandelier, specially made for the pub when it was refurbished a few years back. The south wall is entirely devoted to certificates the pub has won for its floral arrangements, arranged either side of a stained-glass window depicting – you guessed it – a clock. If you visit the pub in winter there are photos on display to tempt you back to see the flowers in full bloom in the summer.

Above and below: A grand and imposing Victorian building with a heart of gold and buckets of charm. On a clear summer's day lovely views of Peckham Rye can be enjoyed from the outdoor seating, while in winter the bounty of clocks inside are an equally pleasant distraction.

The Clock House is a delightful spot on a sunny day, enjoying views of the gently rising slope of Peckham Rye. This comprises some 64 acres of ancient commonland opened as a park in 1894, next to a further 49 acres of Peckham Rye Park. William Blake claimed to have seen a vision of angels in an oak tree on Peckham Rye as a child, and Elizabeth Cadbury, the Quaker and wife of George Cadbury of chocolate fame, lived in a house overlooking the common as a girl.

THE CROWN & GREYHOUND

ADDRESS: 73 DULWICH VILLAGE, SE21
BEERS: BASS, ADNAM'S BITTER, TETLEY
HOURS: MON–SAT 11AM–11PM; SUN 12 NOON–10.30PM

Many parts of London like to think of themselves as villages, but Dulwich Village is the real thing, even down to its unique white wooden finger-posts. Dulwich has managed to retain its village identity thanks to strict control over development exerted by the Dulwich Estate. The extensive grounds of Dulwich College, which was once attended by the young Lord Byron, dominate the village. The college is the principal landowner, raising a levy on local businesses, of which The Crown & Greyhound is one.

This large pub with its huge garden is the focal point of the village, not least because there is not another half-decent pub for quite a distance in any direction. It was not always thus, however. The pub's unusual name derives from the fact that Dulwich once had two inns: The Crown, on the present site, was a small weatherboarded alehouse where farm labourers would stop to rest after a day's work in the fields; The Greyhound was directly opposite and, being the haunt of local gentlemen, was a much grander affair altogether. The Greyhound could host balls, and the Dulwich Club – founded in 1772 – met there for dinners which included such delicacies as 'hunting pudding', 'turtle supe' and 'mins pys'. Charles Dickens attended Dulwich Club dinners, as did many celebrities of the day. When the time came to say farewell to The Greyhound it was decided, in true Dulwich style, to minimize the disruption by altering the name of the Crown.

A short distance from the pub, between the college and the almshouses both founded by Edward Alleyn, a famous Elizabethan actor and contemporary of Shakespeare – is the Dulwich Picture Gallery, the area's principal attraction. It is the world's oldest public art gallery and was the brainchild of French picture dealer Noël Desenfans, his wife Margaret and their friend the landscape painter Sir Francis Bourgeois. Desenfans had put together a collection for Stanislas Augustus, King of Poland, but when the king was forced to abdicate Desenfans found himself the unexpected owner of the lot. The gallery was opened in 1817 – 21 years before the National Gallery – and contains among its 600-strong collection works by Rembrandt, Murillo, Van Dyck, Canaletto and Cornelius Bol. The gallery was designed by the leading architect of the day, Sir John Soane, and is regarded as a masterpiece as it allows the pictures to be viewed in the maximum of natural light.

The founders are buried in a mausoleum attached to the gallery, the cupola of which inspired another leading architect, Sir Gilbert Scott, when designing the shape of London's famous red telephone boxes.

Above and left: Known to locals as 'The Dog', the impressive Crown & Greyhound stands alongside Dulwich College and Dulwich Picture Gallery as the third of the village's great institutions.

THE DOG AND BELL

ADDRESS: 116 PRINCE STREET, SE8
BEERS: FULLER'S LONDON PRIDE, FULLER'S ESB, BRAKSPEAR'S SPECIAL, GUEST ALES
HOURS: MON–SAT 12 NOON–11PM; SUN 12 NOON–4PM, 7PM–10.30PM

Exclusivity always brings a certain extra enjoyment to any experience. It may come about as a result of selection (price, class, membership) or just happenstance. Frequently the best things in life are hard to find. George Orwell famously wrote about the perfect pub, which he called the Moon Under Water. The moon reflected in water is an intangible thing, and so, sadly, Orwell's pub never existed. Closer to hand, however, but definitely off the beaten track, is The Dog and Bell, and while no one would claim it is a perfect pub a visit is a considerably better use of time than a lifetime's search for the impossible.

A combination of those two magical ingredients, a real-ale pub and an honest-to-goodness locals' pub, The Dog and Bell is tucked away in a warren of Deptford's riverside streets, between the largely deserted former naval yard at Convoys Wharf and a recreation ground called, bizarrely, Twinkle Park. A regular entry in the Campaign For Real Ale's *Good Beer Guide* – the drinkers' bible – it has been lauded by the campaign as its south-east London pub of the year.

This one-bar pub displays its credentials in the shape of pump clips from well-drunk guest ales over the bar, and on its walls are a collection of rag-tag notices from locals which may range from a request for studio space from a pair of artists to the latest newspaper cutting charting the career of local-boy-made-good Jools Holland. Church-pew seating around the walls and high-backed chairs at the bar invite customers to sprawl. The energetically minded can play bar billiards, and outdoor types can take advantage of the walled beer garden. The River Thames is nearby, as is Deptford Market. Sunday night is the pub's quiz night.

Above and right: This award-winning dockers' alehouse is particularly well thought of among beer aficionados and locals.

THE GEORGE INN

ADDRESS: 77 BOROUGH HIGH STREET, SE1
BEERS: GEORGE ALE, GREENE KING ABBOT ALE, FULLER'S LONDON PRIDE, FLOWERS
HOURS: MON–SAT 11AM–11PM; SUN 12 NOON–10.30PM

Without a shadow of doubt The George Inn is the most important pub in London, in that it is the last surviving Southwark galleried inn. There is much more history associated with The George than space here could even start to do justice to. So much so that its owners – the National Trust – have written a book laying out the story of The George, so the best advice is to go there and read it. Both William Shakespeare and Charles Dickens are known to have drunk here, and pretty much anyone who has been anyone has paid it a visit at one time or another.

Most famous of the Southwark inns was, of course, Geoffrey Chaucer's Tabard Inn, as depicted in his famous *The Canterbury Tales*, and the galleried portion of The George gives some idea of what The Tabard would have looked like. They were just two of many inns that crowded back to back – hence the galleries – along Borough High Street. Borough High Street was London's most important thoroughfare when London Bridge was the only connection between London (exclusively on the north of the river) and Southwark. Southwark was where Londoners played, as being outside the City it escaped many of the City's ordinances. Hence, all the theatres, the bull and bear rings and the brothels, or stews, were all located in Southwark.

The George's origins are obscure, but it was well estab-

lished by the reign of Henry VIII (1509–47) and we know that one Nicholas Marten was landlord in 1558. In 1670 a fire which started in the rope store demolished part of the structure, and another fire in 1676 destroyed The George and another 500 Southwark dwellings. So, the oldest part of the inn is actually the ungalleried portion which was rebuilt after the fire, though the galleried part is also 17th-century and once extended to the two other sides of the courtyard.

The real business of inns like The George was wag-goning – moving freight around the country in the days before rail. As centres of commerce the inns themselves became wealthy establishments, and as the nation's roads improved the significance of the trade improved too. The George added stage-coaching to the

waggoning trade in the 18th century, but never became one of the top-quality coaching inns. Sadly the trade from both these businesses declined with the rise of the railways. This is why the lease on The George was only £6 per annum in 1828 but £150 per annum in 1668.

In the end, all the great Southwark inns fell victim to the railways, and Chaucer's Tabard Inn was demolished by property developers in 1875 despite a public outcry. Ironically, The George survived because it was bought by a railway, the Great Northern Railway Company, in 1873, who used the courtyard as a goods clearing yard for parcels and freight items moved by train. This function resulted in the destruction of the north and east galleries; the south side was saved only by the tenacity of the tenant.

The advent of the motorcar spelt the end of The George's function as an inn, but by this time its remarkable history and status were starting to be more widely appreciated, and in 1937 it was gifted to the National Trust, who took it over to ensure that we can continue to enjoy its many rooms and many pleasures today.

Below left and below: Named after England's patron saint, this ancient galleried coaching inn is a true survivor and as such is one of England's national treasures.

THE GREENWICH UNION

ADDRESS: 50 ROYAL HILL, SE10
BEERS: BLONDE BEER, HOUSE ALES
HOURS: MON–SAT 11AM–11PM; SUN 12 NOON–10.30PM

Immediately next door to the traditional-looking Richard I (see page 153) is one of London's newest pubs. The Greenwich Union is named after a beer – Union – brewed by the Meantime Brewing Co. Ltd, which is also situated in Greenwich, and this is the first tied house of Britain's fastest-growing brewery firm. All the beers served come from the brewery, and the pub is unique in London for selling no national brewery products whatsoever, not even Guinness. The brewery is the brainchild of Brewmaster Alastair Hook, who trained at the world-famous brewing school at Weihenstephen near Munich in Bavaria (also home to the world's oldest brewery, dating back to 1044).

The Greenwich Union is an attempt at a fusion of the traditional pub and the contemporary bar, aiming to create the relaxed atmosphere of the pub with the emphasis on service and friendliness that many modern bars offer and which is increasingly central to the success of any commercial operation. The result is that the Union has developed a keen following in a remarkably short period of time.

The long, thin pub opens out to a light, airy conservatory and a secluded beer garden. The pub has given a new young chef carte blanche to make his name, and sources ingredients for its dishes from the cheese shop, organic butcher and the fishmonger on this village street. The emphasis on local foods and local beers is one that consumers appreciate, and the Union uses the awareness of its customers to encourage them to think about beer in terms of food. This often leaves them pleasantly surprised.

If you ask for a taster set you will be given a sample of each of the beers to try before you settle on your favourite. In the chocolate stout, the raspberry beer and the wheat beer you will discover tastes and styles that will almost certainly be new to you. This is cutting-edge brewing and pub service, presented by people whose passion about the quality of their offering is infectious.

Above and left: *The Greenwich Union could be described as an alehouse of the future: it shuns national brewery products, preferring to champion high-quality lager and its own beer.*

THE HORSESHOE INN

ADDRESS: 26 MELIOR STREET, SE1
BEERS: FULLER'S LONDON PRIDE, BRAKSPEAR'S BITTER
HOURS: MON–SAT 11AM–11PM; SUN 12 NOON–10.30PM

If you were to enter Melior Street from Fenning Street and look to your right, a bleak wall of brick and glass would stretch up before you, blocking out the sky. This is Guy's Hospital, framed by the varying shades of blue steel and grey and brown brick of half a dozen formless office blocks. Turn to your left by way of contrast and the prospect of The Horseshoe Inn looks joyously welcoming. It even says 'Welcome' in plaster-work over the door.

Built in 1897 it stands on the site of an old coaching inn, remnants of which are still visible. The garden, known locally as 'the oasis', is built over the old stables, whose foundations have been preserved for future archaeological reference. The garden is home to a particularly poisonous plant – belladonna, or deadly nightshade – and in years gone by Guy's Hospital was known to have used it as a source for various preparations and drugs.

The Horseshoe is a good example of a backstreet local, and has the look of a place that is well cared for – which is the key to what marks a good pub from the run of the mill. Food is traditional pub grub served in the bar or in the neat and tidy dining room.

Despite its out-of-the-way location, it attracts a fair following from far and wide. For example, there is a steady stream of Americans who come to visit Fern, the pub's dog, who enjoyed celebrity by being written about in a US magazine. The pub has been used as a television location on several occasions and as such is a favourite haunt of TV types when in the area.

Consistently popular with the staff of Guy's Hospital, it is also handy for those working for the Mayor of London in his new riverside offices. The pub is close to the host of diverse London attractions that are collected between London and Tower bridges, including Borough Market, the London Dungeon and the Design Museum.

Above and below: The Horseshoe Inn is a serendipitous find, being just a yard or two too far from the attractions of Tooley Street and London Bridge to have been spoilt by developers looking to make a quick buck.

THE KINGS ARMS

ADDRESS: 25 ROUPELL STREET, SE1

BEERS: BRAKSPEAR'S BITTER, ADNAM'S BITTER, MARSTON'S PEDIGREE, TETLEY

HOURS: MON–SAT 11AM–11PM; SUN 12 NOON–10.30PM

A lovely little backstreet boozer in a terrace of immaculate Georgian two-up-two-downs, just to the rear of Waterloo East Station, The Kings Arms is a very stylish operation and a wonderful example of the difference a little care and attention to detail can make.

The pub is unusual in that it is one of the few to have resisted the temptation to knock the public and saloon bars together; they remain separated by a two-thirds-height wooden partition, adding to the cosy feeling on either side. The long public bar gets less natural light and consequently has a slightly darker feel, but it is tastefully decorated with a range of photographs of Roupell Street in years gone by. The saloon is more open, with a more eclectic range of decoration; the windows advertise the pub's continuous inclusion in the *Good Beer Guide*.

To the rear of the public bar is a dining room where Thai food is a speciality. The room is split between tables on the left and counter and stool seating along the walls; it is a pleasant and fun space under a conservatory roof and with a range of well-chosen clutter. Food is served until 10pm Monday to Friday, and it is clear that there are a number of South Bank regulars who have worked out that The Kings Arms is a good thing.

There is no shortage of things to see and do within a very easy walk of Roupell Street, and considering the paucity of decent pubs nearer the main tourist attractions, you would be well advised to make a beeline for The Kings Arms after a concert at the Royal Festival Hall or the Queen Elizabeth Hall. Similarly lacking a good pub closer at hand are the National Theatre, the National Film Theatre, the Museum of the Moving Image, the Hayward Gallery, the London Eye, the London Aquarium and the Imax cinema. In the other direction both the Young and the Old Vic are not too far.

Above and below: This charming little two-bar pub was once a funeral directors, but all sombreness has long since been replaced with charm.

THE MARKET PORTER

ADDRESS: 9 STONEY STREET, SE1
BEERS: COURAGE BEST, HARVEY'S SUSSEX BITTER, GUEST ALES
HOURS: MON–FRI 7.30AM–9AM, 11AM–11PM; SAT 11AM–11PM; SUN 12 NOON–10.30PM

There are four world-class 'ale' pubs in London: The White Horse in south-west London (see page 122), The Wenlock Arms in north London (see page 108), The Priory Arms in south-west London (see page 133) and The Market Porter in the south-east. Each is distinguished by an absolute belief in the wondrous qualities of a good pint of traditional English ale, and each ensures that its customers are provided with a constantly varying selection of the best of British.

The Market Porter is possibly the *primus inter pares* (first among equals) of this illustrious group in terms of the sheer range and variety of beers it offers. As the most centrally located and with a guaranteed seven-day-a-week trade, its ales turn over faster and therefore change faster too.

There has been a pub on the site since 1638, at which time it would have been one of scores of alehouses and inns clustered along Borough High Street in the days when London Bridge was the only crossing on the River Thames to the City of London. The Market Porter's proximity to Southwark Cathedral would also have brought it business, as would have the nearby Hop Exchange, where the hop crops from Kent, Sussex and Hampshire were traded and from which the many breweries gathered along the south bank of the Thames would have bought their supplies; there, too – thanks to the wild fluctuations in hop crop yields – fortunes were made and lost by speculators.

Today it is Borough Market that provides the lifeline, and as one of London's two remaining central markets (the other being Smithfield) Borough has ensured that the surrounding neighbourhood has remained largely unchanged. Any regular to The Market Porter will have seen film crews working in Park Street, which is still the most 'Dickensian-looking' street in London. The pub opens at 7.30am to cater for the market traders and closes again at 9am. Farmers' markets at the weekend keep the trade going, and even Sundays are busy with people travelling to the pub just to sample beers that they cannot get in the pubs near where they work or live.

Above right and right: It is very rare to catch this pub in a quiet moment, as it caters not only for Borough Market's traders and visitors but also for the numerous film crews who practically queue up to use characterful Park Street.

THE MAYFLOWER

ADDRESS: 117 ROTHERHITHE STREET, SE16
BEERS: GREENE KING IPA, GREENE KING ABBOT ALE
HOURS: MON–SAT 12 NOON–11PM; SUN 12 NOON–10.30PM

This handsome old house was originally named either The Spread Eagle & Crown or The Shippe (authorities differ), but changed its name in 1957 – ensuring its survival – to The Mayflower, in memory of Captain Christopher Jones. Jones was a Rotherhithe man, who moored his ship *The Mayflower* nearby prior to its departure to collect religious refugees determined to make new lives in the New World in 1620. Rotherhithe was a likely place to find a ship prepared to make such a voyage, as both it and the neighbouring parish of Southwark were known as Dissenting strongholds in the early 17th century.

The pub itself dates from the 16th century, though the present structure is some 200 years younger. Sadly, the upper floor was blown off and destroyed in the Blitz, and the pub was further converted during the 1960s. Yet today it still has a 17th-century feel to it, and if you took the bar and all the trappings away it could resemble a Dissenters' prayer hall. Settle seats are inscribed with words of wit and wisdom;

walls are adorned with *Mayflower* memorabilia and prints of Rotherhithe from the days when it was a residential area supplying labour to the timber trade in Surrey Docks. Due to the fire risk the timber business was not welcome on the north side of the river and, accordingly, a whole quarter grew up around the trade. Until recently the pub doubled as a post office for the convenience of local sailors and, thanks to its American associations, it is still possible to buy American stamps here.

The Mayflower enjoys a riverside location, and a patio on piles driven into the riverbed extends out over the water. Captain Jones returned from his epic voyage in 1621, but tragically died shortly afterwards; he is buried in the neighbouring St Mary the Virgin Church. Next door to the pub is the engine room of the Rotherhithe Tunnel, which contains a working steam engine and exhibition.

Above, opposite and below: The Mayflower has been a veritable institution in Rotherhithe for four centuries thanks to its prime riverside location.

PILOT INN

ADDRESS: RIVER WAY, SE10
BEERS: YOUNG'S BITTER, FULLER'S LONDON PRIDE, FULLER'S ESB, MORLAND'S OLD SPECKLED HEN
HOURS: MON–SAT 11AM–11PM; SUN 12 NOON–10.30PM

The Irish proprietor of the Pilot Inn, Phillip Marron, is a shrewd man. Prior to the construction of the ill-fated Millennium Dome he was offered a large amount of money for his pub in order that the property developers could demolish it; he said 'No'. Herein lies a happy tale, as great pubs survive and survivors make great pubs.

Built in 1801, the Pilot's sign depicts the familiar orange-painted launch of a Thames pilot, the freelance navigators whose local knowledge ensures the safe passage of vessels into estuaries and rivers. However, some say that it was so called because it was built on land owned by William Pitt the Younger, prime minister from 1783 to 1801 and from 1804 to 1806, who was nicknamed the Pilot. A mix of half-timbered rooms and a large, sheltered, sunken garden make this a great pub.

During the construction of the Millennium Dome it was thronged with stocking-footed building workers who all left their muddy boots outside the door, and during the Dome's short and frantic life it was crowded with energetic dancers, acrobats and performers. Now that the Dome is empty, the pub is still full. People seem to arrive from nowhere like mushrooms in the night, reminding you, at lunchtimes, that there are quite a few businesses in the area and at weekends that there are plenty of south London families prepared to travel to a good pub. As the area from the Dome to Woolwich is set to receive an unprecedented level of investment in the next few years, it would seem that the Pilot Inn is set to play an increasingly significant role as the great community local.

The North Greenwich peninsula is gradually getting the kind of development that it needs and houses are gradually inching their way towards the Pilot's door, meaning that Phillip Marron is set to continue to reap the rewards of refusing to succumb to the developers' wallets.

Left: This unassuming pub is capable of holding quite large numbers both inside and out, hence its popularity as a Sunday lunch venue among many south London families.

THE RICHARD I

ADDRESS: 52–54 ROYAL HILL, SE10
BEERS: YOUNG'S BITTER, YOUNG'S SPECIAL, YOUNG'S TRIPLE A
HOURS: MON–SAT 11AM–11PM; SUN 12 NOON–10.30PM

Ask a Greenwich resident to direct you to the best pub around and they will direct you to the Tolly, as The Richard I is affectionately known. Originally two 18th-century shops, one selling sweets and the other beer, the premises were acquired by the Tollemache and Cobbold Brewery of Ipswich and knocked together some time between 1920 and 1923. Young's Brewery added it to their portfolio as a far-flung outpost of their south-west London empire in 1974 during one of those periods of pub estate churning that goes on from time to time, but it is still known as the Tolly.

Royal Hill is the road up to the more genteel parts of Greenwich, and the pub certainly benefits from its seclusion. It is definitely the place to come for conversation or quiet contemplation of the newspaper without distraction or interruption. If you have not been before, choose the right-hand door into the main bar; the left-hand door is strictly for a select band of locals. If you can, grab the distinctive bay-window seat, which gives you a bird's-eye view of what is happening on Royal Hill. If it is sunny lose yourself in the large beer garden, which operates a popular barbecue at weekends.

The Richard I is a great jumping-off point for Greenwich's many treasures. The 190-acre Greenwich Park, enclosed by the Duke of Gloucester between 1417 and 1437, is three minutes away. At the top of the hill in the park is the world-famous observatory, the foundation stone of which was laid in 1675. From the observatory you can look out at one of the best views of London; in the foreground is the Queen's House built for Anne of Denmark, wife of James I (1566–1625). The Queen's House stands in front of the former Royal Naval College built by Sir Christopher Wren, Nicholas Hawksmoor and Sir John Vanbrugh; the college stands on the site of the old Greenwich Palace, the favourite home of the Tudors and birthplace of Henry VIII in 1491, Mary I in 1516 and Elizabeth I in 1533.

Above and right: Lovingly known by most locals as the Tolly, this 18th-century pub is a rare east London outlet of south-west London brewers Young's.

THE ROYAL OAK

ADDRESS: 44 TABARD STREET, SE1
BEERS: HARVEY'S SUSSEX BITTER, HARVEY'S PALE ALE, HARVEY'S MILD, HARVEY'S ARMADA
HOURS: MON–FRI 11AM–11PM

As the sole London outlet of Sussex brewers Harvey's of Lewes, The Royal Oak is very much a magnet for beer lovers as well as representing a sympathetic rescue of a fine and unusual Victorian interior. Harvey's occupies an usual place in the pantheon of UK brewers in that – along with Timothy Taylor's of Yorkshire – it is the most widely admired and respected within the brewing trade. When, in 1999, the River Ouse burst its banks and inundated the brewery, other rival brewers rallied round, offering casks, assistance with saving the yeast strain and – significantly – not poaching accounts when the brewery was down. As a result Harvey's,

founded in 1790, was back in production in a remarkably short time, and its ardent band of followers could breathe a sigh of relief. The Jenner family who run the firm have had their share of adversity in recent years. The brewery was ravaged by fire only a few years before the flood. A plague of frogs is expected any time.

Harvey's Sussex Bitter is occasionally available in some of London's better beer establishments, but given the restricted choice offered by the vast bulk of London's hostelries, a pub offering the full range is a boon, and the chance of drinking them in such pleasant surroundings is an added bonus – the cast-iron pillars and ceiling plasterwork are original.

The entrance on Nebraska Street opens onto an office window in the bar, with a door to the saloon bar to the left and onto the public bar on the right, creating a separation of the kind that is now pretty rare. Pale eggshell walls in the public bar and richer burgundy colours in the saloon bar are judiciously hung with prints. In the public bar the prints are of a theatrical nature, reflecting the dramatic interests of brewery boss Miles Jenner. In the saloon the brewery itself is well represented.

Drinkers in the public bar have the odd sensation of looking at the back of the bar of the saloon as there is no corresponding frontage at head height. The sweeping lines created are very effective.

A little off the beaten track, perhaps, but the pub is still well situated to act as a staging post when exploring historic Southwark, and with Little Dorrit Street, Copperfield Street and Quilp Street all nearby the area's literary connections are not in doubt. Guy's Hospital, Vinopolis, Southwark Cathedral and the Tate Modern are all within reasonable walking distance. In the other direction the Imperial War Museum is a 10-minute walk.

Left: Beer is the main attraction here, as this is the only public house in London that sells the full range of ales produced by respected Sussex brewers Harvey's. The Royal Oak is unusual in having retained its distinct public and saloon bars.

TRAFALGAR TAVERN

◆

ADDRESS: 5 PARK ROW, SE10
BEERS: COURAGE BEST, FLAGSHIP BITTER
HOURS: MON–SAT 11AM–11PM; SUN 12 NOON–10.30PM

I t is hard to contemplate, but only a little over 200 years ago Greenwich was a fishing village, and, in season, one of the catches yielded up by the River Thames was whitebait. Nowadays the River Thames is not quite so prolific, but the Trafalgar Tavern is still *the* place in London to go and eat a whitebait dinner. In the 19th century senior Liberals and Tories would annually board rival barges and sail down the Thames for such a dinner.

At the Trafalgar these dinners would have taken place in what is now the Lord Nelson Room, which offers a view of the broad sweep of the Thames as it embraces the Isle of Dogs. To the powerful leaders of the world's largest empire – from whose far-flung corners raw materials of all sorts came and to where the finished goods were sent – the numbers of ships passing beneath the Trafalgar's bay windows must have been a truly gratifying sight. The view fom the Trafalgar today is still impressive, albeit quite different.

The Trafalgar was built in 1837 by Joseph Kay, a founder member of the Royal Institute of British Architects and surveyor of Greenwich Hospital, on the site of a tavern called The George. It ceased being a pub in 1915, when it became a club named the Royal Alfred Aged Merchant Seamen's Institute. Fortunately, in 1965 it reverted to being the Trafalgar once more. Given that even today great and historic pubs and their interiors are not being retained, the Trafalgar's story must count as one of the most remarkable restorations in London's history.

Above and below: Fans of Charles Dickens should recognize the Trafalgar Tavern from the wedding feast described in Our Mutual Friend.

ADDRESSES & FOOD-SERVING TIMES

◆

THE WEST END

The Argyll Arms
18 Argyll St, W1
Tel: 020 7734 6117
Food: 11am–3pm

The Champion
13 Wells Street, W1
Tel: 020 7323 1228
Food: Mon–Sat
12 noon–2.30pm;
Mon–Thurs 5pm–8.30pm

Cittie of York
22 High Holborn, WC1
Tel: 020 7242 7670
Food: Mon–Sat
12 noon–9pm

The Coach & Horses
29 Greek Street, W1
Tel: 020 7437 5920
Food: Sandwiches only

The Coal Hole
91 Strand, WC1
Tel: 020 7379 9883
Food: 12 noon–5pm

The Cock
27 Great Portland Street, W1
Tel: 020 7631 5002
Food: Mon–Fri
12 noon–2.30pm;
Mon–Thurs 6pm–8.30pm

The Cross Keys
31 Endell Street, WC2
Tel: 020 7836 5185
Food: 12 noon–2.30pm

The Dog & Duck
18 Bateman Street, W1
Tel: 020 7494 0697
Food: None available

The Dover Castle
43 Weymouth Mews, W1
Tel: 020 7580 4412
Food: Mon–Fri 12 noon–
2.30pm, 6pm–9.30pm

The Fitzroy Tavern
16 Charlotte Street, W1
Tel: 020 7580 3714
Food: 12 noon–2.30pm,
7.30pm–9.30pm

The French House
49 Dean Street, W1
Tel: 020 7437 2799
Food: Mon–Sat 12 noon–
3pm, 6pm–10.30pm

The Guinea
30 Bruton Place, W1
Tel: 020 7409 1728
Food: Mon–Fri
12.30pm–2.30pm

Hand & Racquet
48 Whitcomb Street, WC2
Tel: 020 7930 5905

Food: Mon–Sat
12 noon–6pm

The Lamb
94 Lamb's Conduit Street,
WC1
Tel: 020 7405 0713
Food: Mon–Sat
12 noon–2.30pm,
6pm–9pm;
Sun 12 noon–2.30pm

Lamb and Flag
33 Rose Street, WC2
Tel: 020 7497 9504
Food: 12 noon–3pm

The Marquis of Granby
51 Chandos Place, WC2
Tel: 020 7836 7657
Food: 12 noon–3pm

Newman Arms
23 Rathbone Street, W1
Tel: 020 7636 1127
Food: Mon–Thurs
12 noon–3pm, 6–9pm;
Fri 12 noon–3pm

The Porterhouse
21–22 Maiden Lane, WC2
Tel: 020 7836 9931
Food: Mon–Sat 12 noon–
9pm; Sun 12 noon–5pm

Princess Louise
208 High Holborn, WC1
Tel: 020 7405 8816
Food: 12 noon–2.30pm,
6.30–8.30pm

Queens Larder
1 Queen Square, WC1
Tel: 020 7837 5627
Food: 12 noon–8pm

The Red Lion
Crown Passage, SW1
Tel: 020 7930 4141
Food: Sandwiches only

The Red Lion
2 Duke of York Street, SW1
Tel: 020 7321 0782
Food: Mon–Fri 12 noon–
3pm; Sat 12 noon–5pm

The Red Lion
48 Parliament Street, SW1
Tel: 020 7930 5826
Food: 12 noon–2.30pm

The Red Lion
1 Waverton Street, W1
Tel: 020 7499 1307
Food: Mon–Fri 12 noon–
3pm, 6pm–9.30pm; Sat
6pm–9.30pm; Sun 12
noon–3pm, 6pm–9.30pm

The Salisbury
90 St Martin's Lane, WC2
Tel: 020 7836 5863

Food: Mon–Sat
12 noon–10.30pm;
Sun 12 noon–10pm

The Seven Stars
53 Carey Street, WC2
Tel: 020 7242 8521
Food: Mon–Fri
11am–3.30pm; Sat all day

The Sherlock Holmes
10–11 Northumberland
Street, WC2
Tel: 020 7930 2644
Food: 12 noon–10pm

The Ship & Shovell
1–3 Craven Passage, WC2
Tel: 020 7839 1311
Food: Mon–Fri 12
noon–3pm; Sat 12
noon–4pm

Star & Garter
62 Poland Street, W1
Tel: 020 7439 2787
Food: Sandwiches only

THE CITY & THE EAST END

The Black Friar
174 Queen Victoria
Street, EC4
Tel: 020 7236 5474
Food: Mon–Fri
12 noon–2.30pm

The Black Lion
Plaistow High Street, E13
Tel: 020 8472 2351
Food: Mon–Fri 12 noon–
2.15pm, 5pm–7.30pm

The Cockpit
7 St Andrews Hill, EC4
Tel: 020 7248 7315
Food: Mon–Fri 12 noon–
2.30pm, 5pm–8.30pm

Dickens Inn
St Katharine's Dock, E1
Tel: 020 7488 2208
Food: 12 noon–9.30pm

The Fox & Anchor
115 Charterhouse Street,
EC1
Tel: 020 7253 5075
Food: Mon–Fri 7am–2pm

The Grapes
76 Narrow Street, E14
Tel: 020 7987 4396
Food: Mon–Fri 12 noon–
2pm, 7pm–9pm; Sat 12
noon–2.30pm, 7pm–9pm;
Sun 12 noon–3pm

The Hand & Shears
1 Middle Street, EC1
Tel: 020 7600 0257
Food: Mon–Sat
12 noon–3pm

The Harlequin
27 Arlington Way, EC1
Food: Mon–Thurs
12 noon–7pm;
Fri 12 noon–5pm

Hoop & Grapes
47 Aldgate High Street, EC3
Tel: 020 7265 5171
Food: Mon–Fri
12 noon–3pm

The Hope
94 Cowcross Street, EC1
Tel: 020 7250 1442
Food: Mon–Fri
7am–10am, 12 noon–2pm

The Jerusalem Tavern
55 Britton Street, EC1
Tel: 020 7490 4281
Food: Mon–Fri
12 noon–3pm

Lamb Tavern
Leadenhall Market, EC3
Tel: 020 7626 2454
Food: 12 noon–2pm

The Old Bell
95 Fleet Street, EC4
Tel: 020 7583 0216
Food: Mon–Fri
12 noon–3pm

Old Red Lion
418 St John Street, EC4
Tel: 020 7833 3053
Food: Soup & sandwiches

The Pride of Spitalfields
3 Heneage Street, E1
Tel: 020 7247 8933
Food: Mon–Fri
12 noon–2pm

Punch Tavern
99 Fleet Street, EC4
Tel: 020 7353 6658
Food: Mon–Fri
12 noon–3pm

The Royal Oak
73 Columbia Road,
Tel: 020 7739 8204
Food: Sun 8am–2pm

The Three Kings
7 Clerkenwell Close, EC1
Tel: 020 7253 0483
Food: Mon–Fri
12 noon–2.30pm

The Viaduct Tavern
126 Newgate Street, EC1
Tel: 020 7600 1863
Food: Sandwiches only

Ye Olde Cheshire Cheese
Wine Office Court, 145
Fleet Street, EC4
Tel: 020 7353 6170
Food: Mon–Sat

12 noon–9pm;
Sun 12 noon–3pm

Ye Olde Mitre Tavern
Ely Place, EC1
Tel: 020 7405 4751
Food: Sandwiches only

MARYLEBONE TO BELGRAVIA

Anglesea Arms
15 Selwood Terrace, SW7
Tel: 020 7373 7960
Food: Mon–Fri 12 noon–
3pm, 6.30pm–10pm;
Sat–Sun 12 noon–10pm;
Sun 6pm–9.30pm

The Antelope
22 Eaton Terrace, SW1
Tel: 020 7824 8512
Food: Mon–Sat
12 noon–2pm

The Archery Tavern
4 Bathurst Street, W2
Tel: 020 7402 4916
Food: 12 noon–2.45pm,
6pm–9pm (except Fri eves)

The Barley Mow
8 Dorset Street, W1
Tel: 020 7935 7318
Food: Mon–Sat
12 noon–3pm

Duke of Wellington
94 Crawford Street, W1
Tel: 020 7224 9435
Food: Mon–Fri 12 noon–
3pm; Wed–Fri 6pm–9pm;
Sun 12 noon–4pm.

The Feathers
43 Linhope Street, NW1
Tel: 020 7402 1327
Food: Mon–Fri
12 noon–3pm

The Grenadier
Old Barrack Yard, Wilton
Row, SW1
Tel: 020 7235 3074
Food: Mon–Fri 12 noon–
2.30pm, 6.30pm–9.30pm;
Sat–Sun 12 noon–9pm

The Nags Head
53 Kinnerton Street, SW1
Tel: 020 7235 1135
Food: 12 noon–9.30pm

The Queen's Arms
30 Queen's Gate Mews,
SW1
Tel: 020 7581 7741
Food: Mon–Sat 12 noon–
8pm; Sun 12 noon–6pm

The Star Tavern
6 Belgrave Mews West, SW1
Tel: 020 7235 3019
Food: Mon–Fri 12 noon–

9pm; Sat–Sun 12 noon–
3pm, 7pm–9pm

The Victoria
10 Strathearn Place, W2
Tel: 020 7724 1191
Food: Mon–Sat 12 noon–
2.30pm, 6pm–9.30pm;
Sun 12 noon–9pm

The Warrington Hotel
93 Warrington Crescent, W9
Tel: 020 7266 3134
Food: 12 noon–2.30pm,
6pm–10.30pm

The Windsor Castle
27–29 Crawford Place, W1
Tel: 020 7723 4371
Food: Sun–Fri 12 noon–
3pm, 6pm–10pm;
Sat 6pm–10pm

NORTH LONDON
The Albert
11 Princess Road, NW1
Tel: 020 7722 1886
Food: Mon–Thurs 12
noon–2.30pm, 6.30pm–
10pm; Fri 12 noon–3pm,
6.30pm–10pm; Sat–Sun
12 noon–10pm

The Albion
10 Thornhill Road, N1
Tel: 020 7607 7450
Food: Mon–Fri 12 noon–
3pm, 6pm–10pm; Sat 12
noon–10pm; Sun 12
noon–5pm, 6pm–9.15pm

The Assembly House
292–4 Kentish Town
Road, NW5
Tel: 020 7485 2031
Food: 12 noon–6pm

The Camden Head
Camden Passage, N1
Tel: 020 7359 0851
Food: 12 noon–9.30pm

The Flask
14 Flask Walk, NW3
Tel: 020 7435 4580
Food: Mon–Sat 12 noon–
3.30pm; Tues–Sat 6pm–
8.30pm; Sun 12 noon–4pm

Holly Bush
22 Holly Mount, NW3
Tel: 020 7435 2892
Food: Mon–Sat 12.30pm–
4pm, 6pm–10pm

King's Head
115 Upper Street, N1
Tel: 020 7226 0364
Food: Tues–Sat
12 noon–3pm; Eves 1
hour before peformances;
Sun 12 noon–7pm

The Magdala
South Hill Park, N3
Tel: 020 7435 2503

Food: Mon–Fri 12 noon–
2.30pm, 6pm–10pm;
Sat 12 noon–10pm;
Sun 12 noon–9.30pm

O'Reilly's
Kentish Town Road, NW5

The Pineapple
51 Leverton Street, NW5
Tel: 020 7284 4631
Food: 12 noon–3pm,
7pm–10pm

Quinn's
65 Kentish Town Road, N1
Tel: 020 7267 8240
Food: 12 noon–3pm,
6pm–10pm

The Spaniards Inn
Spaniards Road, NW3
Tel: 020 8731 6571
Food: Sun–Fri 12 noon–
3pm, 5pm–8.45pm;
Sat 12 noon–10pm

The Washington
50 England's Lane, NW3
Tel: 020 7722 8842
Food: 12 noon–10pm

The Wenlock Arms
26 Wenlock Road, N1
Tel: 020 7608 3406
Food: Sandwiches only

Ye Olde White Bear
New End, NW3
Tel: 020 7435 3758
Food: 12 noon–9pm

WEST LONDON
Blue Anchor
13 Lower Mall, W6
Tel 020 8748 5774
Food: Mon–Sat 12 noon–
9pm; Sun 12 noon–7.30pm

The Britannia
1 Allen Street, W8
Tel: 020 7937 6905
Food: Mon–Sat 12 noon–
2.45pm, 6pm–9.45pm;
Sun 12 noon–2.45pm,
6pm–9pm

Britannia Tap
150 Warwick Road, W14
Tel: 020 7602 1649
Food: 12 noon–10.30pm

The Bulls Head
15 Thames Road, Strand-
on-the-Green, W4
Tel: 020 8994 1204
Food: All day every day

The Churchill Arms
119 Kensington Church
Street, W8
Tel: 020 7727 4242
Food: Mon–Sat
11am–10pm;
Sun 12 noon–9.30pm

The Cow
89 Westbourne Park Road,
W2
Tel: 020 7221 0021
Food: Mon–Sat 12 noon–
4pm, 6pm–11pm; Sun
6pm–10.30pm

The Dove
19 Upper Mall, W6
Food: Mon–Sat 12 noon–
2pm, 6–9pm; Sun 12
noon–4pm, 6–9pm

Fox & Pheasant
1 Billing Road, SW10
Tel: 020 7352 2943
Food: Mon–Fri
12 noon–2.30pm

The Tabard
Bath Road, W4
Tel: 020 8994 3492
Food: Mon 12 noon–8pm;
Tues–Fri 12 noon–9pm;
Sun 12 noon–6pm

The Warwick Arms
160 Warwick Road, W14
Tel: 020 7603 3560
Food: Mon–Sat
12 noon–12pm;
Sun 12 noon–10.45pm

The White Horse
Parsons Green Lane, SW6
Tel: 020 7736 2115
Food: 12 noon–10pm

The Windsor Castle
114 Campden Hill Road,
W8
Tel: 020 7243 9551
Food: 12 noon–10pm

SOUTH-WEST
LONDON
The Alma
499 Old York Road, SW18
Tel: 020 8870 2537
Food: 12 noon–4pm,
6pm–10.30pm

The Castle
115 Battersea High Street,
SW11
Tel: 020 7228 8181
Food: Mon–Sat 12 noon–
3pm, 7pm–9.45pm;
Sun 12.30pm–4pm,
6pm–9.30pm

The Cat's Back
86–88 Point Pleasant, SW18
Tel: 020 8877 0818
Food: Sun–Fri
12 noon–4pm

The Duke of Cambridge
228 Battersea Bridge
Road, SW11
Tel: 020 7223 5662
Food: Mon–Fri 12 noon–
2.30pm, 7pm–9.45pm;
Sat–Sun 1pm–4pm

The Duke of Devonshire
39 Balham High Road,
SW12
Tel: 020 8673 1363
Food: 12 noon–10pm

Duke's Head
8 Lower Richmond Road,
SW15
Tel: 020 8788 2552
Food: Mon–Fri 11am–
2.30pm, 6pm–10pm;
Sat 11am–10pm;
Sun 12 noon–9pm

The Nightingale
97 Nightingale Lane, SW12
Tel: 020 8673 1637
Food: Mon–Fri 12 noon–
2.15pm, 7pm–9.30pm;
Sat–Sun 1pm–3pm

The Priory Arms
83 Lansdowne Way, SW8
Tel: 020 7622 1884
Food: Mon–Sat
12 noon–2.30pm;
Sun 11.30pm–2.30pm

The Ship
41 Jews Row, SW18
Tel: 020 8870 9667
Food: 12 noon–10.30pm

The Spread Eagle
71 Wandsworth High
Street, SW18
Tel: 020 8877 9809
Food: Mon–Fri
12 noon–2pm

The Woodman
60 Battersea High Street,
SW11
Tel: 020 7228 2968
Food: Mon–Sat 12 noon–
3pm, 6pm–9pm;
Sun 12 noon–6pm

Ye White Hart
The Terrace, Riverside,
SW13
Tel: 020 8876 5177
Food: 12.30–2.30pm,
6.45pm–9.30pm

SOUTH-EAST
LONDON
Anchor Tap
20A Horsleydown Lane,
Bermondsey, SE1
Tel: 020 7403 4637
Food: Mon–Sat 12 noon–
9pm; Sun 12 noon–end

The Clock House
196A Peckham Rye, SE19
Tel: 020 8693 2901
Food: Mon–Fri 12 noon–
2.30pm; Sat–Sun 12
noon–9pm

The Crown & Greyhound
73 Dulwich Village, SE21
Tel: 020 8299 4976
Food: Phone for times

The Dog and Bell
116 Prince Street, SE8
Tel: 020 8692 5664
Food: Mon–Fri 12 noon–
2.30pm, 6pm–9pm

The George Inn
77 Borough High Street, SE1
Tel: 020 7407 2056
Food: Mon–Fri
12 noon–3pm;
Sat–Sun 12 noon–4pm

The Greenwich Union
50 Royal Hill, SE10
Tel: 020 8692 6258
Food: Mon–Sat
12 noon–10pm;
Sun 12 noon–2.30pm;

The Horseshoe Inn
26 Melior Street, SE1
Tel: 020 7403 6364
Food: 12 noon–10pm

The Kings Arms
25 Roupell Street, SE1
Tel: 020 7207 0784
Food: Mon–Fri 12 noon–
3pm, 6pm–10pm;
Sat 6pm–10pm

The Market Porter
9 Stoney Street, SE1
Tel: 020 7407 2495
Food: 11.30am–2.30pm

The Mayflower
117 Rotherhithe Street, SE16
Tel: 020 7237 4088
Food: Tues–Fri 12 noon–
3pm, 6pm–10pm;
Sun 12 noon–4pm

Pilot Inn
River Way, SE10
Tel: 020 8858 5910
Food: Mon–Sat 12 noon–
2.30pm, 6pm–9pm;
Sun 12 noon–4.30pm

The Richard I
52–54 Royal Hill, SE10
Tel: 020 8692 2996
Food: Mon–Sat 12 noon–
2.30pm, 6pm–9pm

The Royal Oak
44 Tabard Street, SE1
Tel: 020 7357 7173
Food: Mon–Fri 12 noon–
2.30pm, 6pm–9.30pm

Trafalgar Tavern
5 Park Row, SE10
Tel: 020 8858 2437
Food: Sun–Mon
12 noon–3pm;
Tues–Sat 12 noon–9pm

INDEX

◆

ACKNOWLEDGEMENTS

◆

Author's acknowledgements:
I would like to extend my sincere thanks to photographer Chris Coe. I count myself lucky that I only had to write about my favourite subject, pubs. Chris had the unenviable task of trying to photograph them during an unusually wet spring and, worse still, during the World Cup, when nearly every pub in England was liveried in flags and bunting. His patience and fortitude, especially when I decided to alter the shortlist, went way beyond anything I could have tolerated. Thanks also to editor Kate Michell for putting up with the world's worst handwriting.

Picture acknowledgements:
Pages 14–15: Courtesy of Fuller Smith & Turner plc